30

BICYCLE TOURS
in New Jersey

30
BICYCLE TOURS
in New Jersey

Almost 1000 Miles of Scenic Pleasures
and Historic Treasures

Arline Zatz

THIRD EDITION

A Backcountry Guide
Woodstock · Vermont

An Invitation to the Reader

Although it is unlikely that the roads you cycle on these tours will change much with time, some road signs, landmarks, and other items may. If you find that changes have occurred on these routes, please let us know so we may correct them in future editions. The author and publisher also welcome other comments and suggestions. Address all correspondence to:

Editor, Bicycle Tours
Backcountry Guides
PO Box 748
Woodstock, Vermont 05091

Library of Congress Cataloging-In Publication Data

Zatz, Arline

30 Bicycle Tours in New Jersey : almost 1000 miles of scenic pleasures and historic treasures / written by Arline Zatz; photographs by Joel Zata. — 2nd Ed.

      p.   cm.

ISBN 0-88150-368-1 (alk. paper)

1. Bicycle touring–New Jersey–Guidebooks. 2. New Jersey–Guidebooks. I. Zatz
Arline. 25 bicycle torus in New Jersey. II. Title.

GV1045.5.N5Z37 1997

917.4904'43–dc21   97-20176

                                                  CIP

Published by Backcountry Guides
A division of The Countryman Press, Inc.
PO Box 748, Woodstock, VT 05091

Distributed by W. W. Norton and Company
500 Fifth Avenue, New York, NY 10110
Cover photo by Brooks Dodge/New England Stock Photo
Cover design by Joanna Bodenweber
Text design by Sally Sherman
Maps by Richard Widhu, © 1998, 1997 Backcountry Guides
Interior photographs by Arline Zatz and Joel L. Zatz

Printed in Canada
10 9 8 7

In memory of my mother, Belle,
who bought me my first wheels,
and my father, Joe, who taught me how to ride.

Acknowledgments

I'd like to express thanks to Backcountry Guides for offering me the opportunity to revise the first edition of *25 Bicycle Tours in New Jersey*. Thanks, too, to my super managing editor, Laura Jorstad, for fine-tuning my words and the maps; to copyeditor Dale Evva Gelfand, for checking details; to the park, museum, and historic site officials who took time out from their busy schedules to document facts; to William Feldman at the New Jersey Department of Transportation, for speedily supplying information; to my friends Laura and Marvin Mausner, for pedaling the extra miles to recheck one of the routes; to Felicia Oliver-Smith, for encouraging me to follow my dream to write the first edition; to Ellen Hulme, for her excellent advice; and to Volvo Cars of North America for the excellent hitch installation on my Volvo, which made it possible to safely transport my bicycle to the various destinations.

Thanks also to my son, Dr. David A. Zatz, for his time, valuable comments, and superior editing skills.

Heartfelt thanks to my friend Mary Elwood, for her encouragement, support, and cherry wishes that helped make my words flow.

And special thanks and lots of love to my husband, Joel, for his role in planning and mapping the original routes, his photographic skills, help with the new maps, and, most of all, the pleasure of his company on each of the rides.

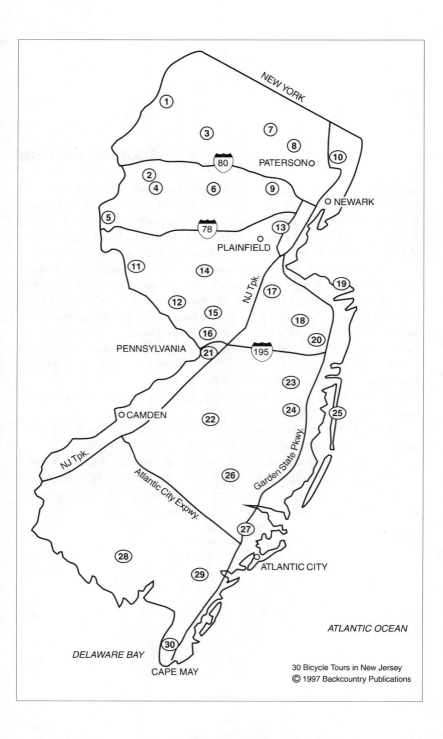

Contents

SOUTHERN NEW JERSEY · 159

Introduction

Learning to ride a two-wheeler at 4 years of age was frightening, exciting, and a memorable experience for me. I can still remember how my father refused to install training wheels. Instead, he preferred running up and down the street holding onto my bicycle seat to balance me. Each time I cried out, begging him to stop because I was afraid of falling, he'd whisper words of encouragement, promising not to let go before I signaled I was ready to pedal on my own.

Eventually he did let go. However, because I was so wrapped up in the thrill of riding my brand-new bicycle, I didn't know the exact moment I had mastered the necessary balance and had pedaled using my own power. Once I was rolling on my own, I felt a great sense of freedom—for I knew I could travel anywhere my wheels could carry me. I loved that bicycle and polished it just about every day, spokes and all. When I finally outgrew it, my mother always managed to muster up some change so that I could rent a bicycle for an hour after school. What joy I felt after graduating from elementary school, for my mother—who had scrimped and saved for ages—surprised me with another brand-new bicycle. I don't think I ever thanked her properly for giving me one of the most wonderful gifts I had ever received, especially since I knew my parents didn't have money to spare, but I'm certain she was aware of the happiness riding that bicycle brought me for years after.

Bicycling—conceived in France in 1790 when Count Made de Sivac linked two wooden wheels with a wooden bridge shaped like a horse's back as a toy for children—is still one of my favorite activities. I can understand why an estimated 3 million people in the Garden State have made this New Jersey's most popular form of outdoor recreation. For openers, bicycling not only reduces stress by refreshing the mind, but it also improves the cardiovascular system, tones the muscles, builds strength and endurance, doesn't degrade the environment, and is inexpensive. It's also lots of fun.

The 30 tours I've laid out cover nearly 1000 miles and explore many of the treasures and delights in the state. No matter which tour you choose, you'll discover New Jersey's great diversity. You can view the state's largest lake in the hilly, northern Skylands section. If you want leisurely pedaling and a perfect example of why New Jersey is known as the Garden State, try a tour through the southern flatlands. The routes traverse lush forests, miles of white sandy beaches, lovely neighborhoods, and natural areas, leading you to historic sites, museums, and wildlife refuges. Rest or fish in the same babbling brooks and flowing rivers that the Lenni-Lenape tribe used, pedal on the same roads General George Washington and his troops traveled upon—and make it a habit to stop frequently to enjoy the special places indicated in each chapter.

To make it easier to choose a tour, the book is divided geographically into three sections: north, central, and south. Trip highlights and information on the county, starting point, terrain, traffic conditions, and distance are listed at the beginning of each tour so that you can see at a glance how difficult the trip is and what you'll encounter along the way. While two of these tours are overnighters, all are circular, and each can be shortened or completed in sections. And if you want to stay overnight, check the listing of hotels, motels, bed & breakfast inns, and campgrounds on pages 218–223 of this book's appendix.

Who These Tours Are For

Whether you ride at a snail's pace or are as fast as a jaguar, whether you're a beginner or an experienced cyclist, you'll find tours here to match your abilities and interests. In choosing a tour, check the terrain rating and mileage from start to finish. If you're out of shape, begin with short, level trips (or parts of longer trips) until you feel comfortable enough to try more difficult ones. By bicycling a couple of times a week, you'll find your ability to venture on slightly hilly terrain has greatly improved.

The Tour

Read each tour carefully a few days before starting out so that you can plan how long to allow for lingering at museums, historic sites, swimming and fishing areas, and so on, and what to bring along. You might also opt to make an overnight reservation at a hotel, motel, bed & breakfast inn, or campground.

Each tour lists in detail where to park your car, turn-by-turn instructions, and running mileage and includes a map showing points of interest.

Local attractions, rest rooms, and food stops are noted in the text; should you need a repair, bicycle repair shops as well as those selling or renting bicycles are noted on pages 224-232 in the appendix. All attractions are fully described, so you can prepare your schedule before you start out. Business hours are given, but since they are subject to change, it's a good idea always to call in advance.

Detailed street maps of each county are available free or at a nominal charge from the respective county offices. Write to the New Jersey Department of Transportation, Pedestrian/Bicycle Advocate, 1035 Parkway Avenue, Trenton, NJ 08625, for a listing.

It's the Law

While bicyclists aren't bogged down by many rules, New Jersey does require that you follow the same rules of the road as car drivers do. In addition to giving hand signals and obeying stop signs, traffic lights, and other warnings, New Jersey law states that:

- Cyclists must remain on the right side of the road except when making a left turn from a left-turn lane, when avoiding drains or other hazardous conditions, or when passing a slower-moving vehicle.
- A red rear reflector and front and rear lights must be used after sunset.
- A bell or horn that can be heard at least 100 feet away must be attached to the bicycle. Sirens or whistles, however, are illegal.
- Children under the age of 14 MUST wear helmets.

Bicycles are not allowed on the Garden State Parkway, New Jersey Turnpike, or Atlantic City Expressway. While interstates in New Jersey are normally closed to bicyclists, most sections may be used by writing for a special permit issued by the New Jersey Department of Transportation (NJDOT), Pedestrian/Bicycle Advocate, 1035 Parkway Avenue, Trenton, NJ 08625. However, none of our routes takes you on the major highways.

Safety Tips

- Always wear a helmet when you ride. You have only one head, and this is its only protection. Today's helmets are light, inexpensive, and provide lots of ventilation. Make certain yours meets Snell, ANSI, or ASTM standards. Fit is essential, too: It shouldn't be too loose. Bright colors are best so that you're easily seen.

- Make yourself visible by wearing bright or light-colored clothing or a simple safety vest.
- Always ride single file, keeping at least three bicycle lengths between you and the cyclist in front.
- Attach a mirror to your helmet, eyeglasses, or handlebars to avoid having to turn your head to look behind. Use a clip or rubber band to keep your pants from becoming tangled in the chain.
- Wear shatterproof sunglasses or goggles to keep insects from flying into your eyes.
- Carry your bicycle across railroad tracks or cross at right angles.
- Test your brakes before a descent.
- If a dog should chase you, keep calm while pedaling. Some cyclists have had success by throwing a cookie off into the distance to distract the dog long enough to make a getaway, while others always carry a canister of Mace or other pepper spray.
- Obey the rules of the road, remembering that you have the same responsibilities as automobiles. Ride WITH traffic, and observe signals, stop, and yield signs.

The Right Bicycle

If you haven't been on a bicycle since you were a kid, you're in for a big surprise. Today, there are hundreds of bicycles to choose from. One-speeds are almost unheard of, as are 3-speeds—the old "English racers." Instead, there's a choice of touring and road bikes (thin tires and curved handlebars, geared for 12 to 24 speeds for going long distances on paved roads), and racing bikes (lightweight and designed specifically for speed). All-terrain mountain bikes have become the rage. Comfortable, tough, with up to 24 speeds, and easy to ride in places that would damage other bicycles, they can go over gravel roads, tree roots, rocks, and shallow water. A hybrid allows you to ride both road and trail, plus it has wider tires than a road bicycle and can haul more weight if you plan to camp.

Prices vary from $200 to $4000, depending on the material and frills, so it pays to do some research. Annual bicycle guides, available at the library or newsstand, will help you narrow the choice. Visit several bicycle shops, ask for test rides, and compare the quality of different brands. Avoid discount stores, which often carry bicycles of inferior quality specifically manufactured to sell at a lower price.

A trailer-hitch-type bike carrier in use

Bicycle Carriers

When driving, instead of cramming your bicycle into the car trunk and risking damage, it's wise to purchase a transport carrier. Three types are available: a *roof rack,* which requires strong muscles to lift the bicycle from the ground to the roof and sometimes a stepladder if you're loading onto a van; a *trunk rack,* which fits onto the back of the trunk, but often causes dents or chipped paint; and the *trailer-hitch-type carrier,* which I use on my Volvo. I've found that this keeps the bicycle(s) a safe distance from the car, holds them high up so they don't scrape the ground when you're backing out of driveways or going over rough road, and prevents damage to the paint. Best of all, the trunk can be opened at any time without having to first remove the bicycle(s).

Before Each Trip
- Inspect and tighten nuts and bolts and lubricate necessary parts.
- Check the tire pressure.
- Adjust the brakes and check the derailleur adjustment.

Reading the Weather

If you're out for a long ride, it's important to know how to read the sky so that you can seek shelter if a storm is brewing. Libraries carry many books on this subject, but remember that thunderstorms often are accompanied by lightning and strong winds, while fog cuts visibility. And if you get too wet, there's always the possibility of hypothermia or frostbite. It's a good idea to check a barometer before any trip, for while steady or rising pressure is usually a sign of good weather ahead, rapidly falling pressure indicates an approaching storm. Should you have the misfortune to be stuck in the middle of a downpour accompanied by lightning, don't take shelter under tall trees or next to a single tree, stay away from wire fences or poles, and, if you're out in an open area, crouch down. A cave, the bottom of a gully, and beneath a large boulder are usually all good bets for seeking shelter.

What to Take

While many of the following items are optional, each is highly recommended:

- Tool kit, spare tube and patch kit, tire irons, gauge, and tire pump. Make certain the pump fits your valves and bicycle frame.
- Lock and chain. Master Lock makes sturdy locks and cables; if weight and price aren't factors, the chainless Kryptonite and Citadel are good bets.
- Filled water bottle and cage. If you're going long distances or it's hot, take a large one or pack two. Remember to drink before you get thirsty to avoid becoming dehydrated.
- Cycling gloves to absorb road shock and protect your hands in case of a fall.
- Cycling jersey for wind resistance and wicking away perspiration.
- Padded shorts or long pants. A synthetic chamois liner helps prevent chafing; quality products contain cushioning in the hip and thigh areas for more protection in case of spills.
- Shoes. Cycling shoes have stiffer soles, but there are differences among those made for touring, racing, and off-road riding.
- Lightweight rain jacket (a poncho can get caught in the wheels).
- Snacks—bananas, grapes, raisins, trail mix, energy bars, oranges— and/or lunch.
- Suntan lotion.

- Insect repellent, when necessary.
- Bandanna.
- Tissues.
- First-aid kit.
- Bathing suit and towel if you're planning to swim.
- Money.
- Knife.
- Panniers to hold extra clothing.
- Camera and film.
- Bird and tree identification books.
- Optional handlebar computer to log distance, speed, and other details.
- Identification bracelet or card in case of an accident.
- Your copy of this book!

Street Smarts

Although I've purposely chosen quiet areas for these trips, there have been times (thankfully rare) when I've encountered rude people who think it's fun to blast a car horn in my ear or toss a beer can at my back. It's natural to feel angry when this happens, but I've learned to stay cool, because safety comes before all else. It's best not to give these idiots the satisfaction of a reaction—which is what they're waiting for. Chalk their behavior up to ignorance and continue on your way, because the rides are refreshing, great exercise, and simply lots of fun.

Emergency Repairs

Checking your bicycle before a tour is the best way to avoid a breakdown. Be familiar with the most common repairs in advance, in case the bicycle breaks down on the road. Buy a repair manual and practice repairing a flat tire or thrown chain at home. Keep a manual in your pannier should you have to make an unexpected repair. (Suggested manuals are listed on page 237 in the appendix.)

New Jersey Tidbits

Size:	Fourth smallest state in the nation
Length:	166 miles from High Point to Cape May
Width:	32 miles at its narrowest point
State motto:	Liberty and Prosperity
State flower:	Purple violet
State bird:	Eastern goldfinch
State animal:	Horse
State insect:	Honeybee
State tree:	Red oak
State dinosaur:	*Hadrosaurus foulkii*
State seashell:	Ribbed whelk
State nickname:	Garden State
State seal:	The Great Seal of New Jersey features the figures of Liberty and Ceres, mythical goddess of prosperity. The plows represent the state's agriculture; the helmet, sovereignty; and the horse, strength in war and commerce.

NORTHERN NEW JERSEY

1
Old Mine Road

Location: *Sussex and Warren Counties*
Starting point: *Millbrook Village, Old Mine Road, Millbrook*
Terrain: *Hilly with some steep climbs*
Traffic: *Very light*
Round-trip distance pedaled: *37.0 miles*
Highlights: *Historic Millbrook Village, scenic Delaware Water Gap region, pedaling on the first road in the nation*

The Lenni-Lenape people discovered the beautiful Delaware River Valley region thousands of years ago and made it their home. Europeans, equally impressed, followed. By the late 19th century, the area became known as a great vacation spot.

Hikers, hunters, bird-watchers, anglers, canoeists, and bicyclists still flock to the 70,000 acres situated on both the Pennsylvania and New Jersey sides of the Delaware River, which is now known as the Delaware Water Gap National Recreation Area. The gap, a distinct notch more than a mile wide, was formed by underground pressure folding the earth's crust and the action of the Delaware River cutting through the Kittatinny Ridge. Exposed rock layers and the folding of the rocks are easily seen in many places.

The route leads through part of the gap and several quiet settlements. Except on summer weekends, traffic is light enough to enjoy the breathtaking natural beauty of the area in solitude. The sometimes strenuous pedaling in hilly terrain is well worth the effort.

Come well supplied with food, drink, and repair tools, since stores are few and far between. It's also a good idea to pick up a park map at the Delaware Water Gap National Recreation Area Visitor Center located on I-80; many roads are unmarked or poorly marked, and town names sometimes vary from one map to another.

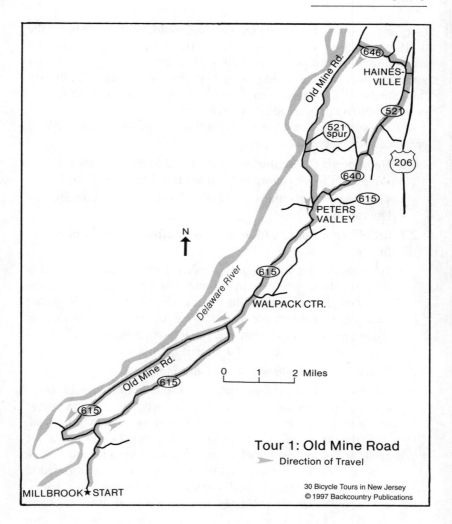

N

Tour 1: Old Mine Road
Direction of Travel

30 Bicycle Tours in New Jersey
© 1997 Backcountry Publications

MILLBROOK ★ START

Park at Millbrook Village, north of the visitors center, and limber up by strolling through this restored crossroads hamlet. Here, National Park Service employees wear period dress and demonstrate handcrafts such as spinning, weaving, and blacksmithing, re-creating a lifestyle that was common in the Delaware River Valley only a generation ago.

The village came to life in 1832 after Abraham Garris built a dam diverting water from a brook to power the wheel of his gristmill. It didn't take long for others to realize that they, too, could make a living near the mill by providing necessary services to the surrounding agricultural community. The village gristmill allowed valley farmers to grind their grain into flour without having to journey over the mountains. Millbrook flourished until 1885, when a railroad line built along the opposite side of the Kittatinny Ridge made it obsolete.

After exploring, bring your bike to the road junction at the village entrance and reset the odometer.

0.0 Head north on (unmarked) River Road toward the town of Walpack. (Some county maps label this Old Mine Road.)

This narrow road climbs steeply uphill before descending sharply. Use caution.

2.1 RIGHT onto Route 615, immediately after crossing a one-lane bridge.

You follow a stream for about 1 mile before encountering a steep section with several choppy up-and-down stretches. Trees stand out like colored lollipops during the fall, affording shade on hot days. As the countryside slopes away, you can catch glimpses of adjoining hills and valleys, and you'll pass through lush, forested areas before reaching the Old Mine Road.

7.4 RIGHT at the T, following the main road.

Food and drink can be purchased at a store in the Walpack Valley Campground on the right just after you make the turn, as well as at the Walpack Inn on your right about 0.5 mile down the road. After the inn, you'll pass a rangers' station on the other side of the road. As you proceed, look out to your right for a beautiful view, especially during the fall. At 11.1 miles, follow the main road to the left as an unmarked road merges from the right.

Peters Valley Craft Village, at the next road junction, is an excellent place to stop, stretch, and examine the fine crafts produced by resident artists working on their specialties. (Free; hours vary.)

11.9 RIGHT onto Route 615, following sign for Route 206.

12.5 LEFT onto Route 640 at a sign for Dingman's Ferry.

There are few houses along this wooded area. Just before the next turn, you'll arrive at a store in the village of Layton.

Journey back in time at Millbrook Village, a restored crossroads hamlet on the Old Mine Road where employees don period dress and demonstrate crafts.

13.8 RIGHT onto Route 521 spur.

14.1 LEFT onto Route 521 North, toward Hainesville.

The road starts uphill, then flattens out.

17.2 LEFT onto unmarked Route 646 at the sign for Old Mine Road.

You'll pass several farms before beginning a steep downhill.

18.8 LEFT at the T onto Old Mine Road.

The Old Mine Road, built by the Dutch in the mid-17th century, was the first road in the United States. Covering 140 miles, it was intended to transport ore from the Pahaquarry copper mine to Esopus (now Kingston, New York) on the Hudson River. From here it was shipped to Holland for smelting.

22.1 STRAIGHT at the junction with Route 521 spur, toward Peters Valley Craft Village.

For about 1 mile this scenic road climbs steeply, but there's relief in the downhill portion, which takes you back to the road junction in Peters Valley.

23.8 STRAIGHT on Route 615 toward Walpack.

28.4 STRAIGHT ahead just past the Walpack Valley Campground onto Old Mine Road.

A marker at 33.7 miles commemorates the building of Old Mine Road.

34.9 RIGHT across the one-lane bridge.

Continue uphill for about 0.6 mile.

37.0 ARRIVE at the entrance to Millbrook Village.

2
A Bit of Hope

Location: *Warren County*
Starting point: *Route 521, just north of I-80, Hope*
Terrain: *Hilly*
Traffic: *Light to moderate*
Round-trip distance pedaled: *25.7 miles*
Highlights: *Exquisite country scenery, historic Hope Village, fishing*

This excursion through rural Warren County takes you through farming country and quiet towns along roads that wind, climb, and—inevitably—descend. In some places you'll get an inkling of what America's most populous state must have been like 50 years ago.

Begin at the **parking** area just north of the I-80 Hope exit, which takes you onto Route 521. Make the first left turn from Route 521 north past the interchange (opposite a motorcycle dealership). If you've passed the police barracks, you've gone too far. Reset your odometer at the parking lot exit adjoining the highway.

0.0 RIGHT onto Route 521 (heading south).

Hope, the first village on the route, is worth slowing down for. The Moravians, a German Protestant sect that came here from Pennsylvania in 1769, built their houses to last. Many of their attractive stone houses still stand, including the Gemeinhaus (community house), the Single Sisters Choir, previously a residence for single women, and the four-and-a-half-story stone mill that had been used for grinding grist.

1.3 RIGHT at the blinker light onto Route 609.

If St. Luke's Episcopal Church is open, stop in for a look at the organ that Queen Anne donated in 1839. Past this point, there are ups and downs on a nearly traffic-free scenic road.

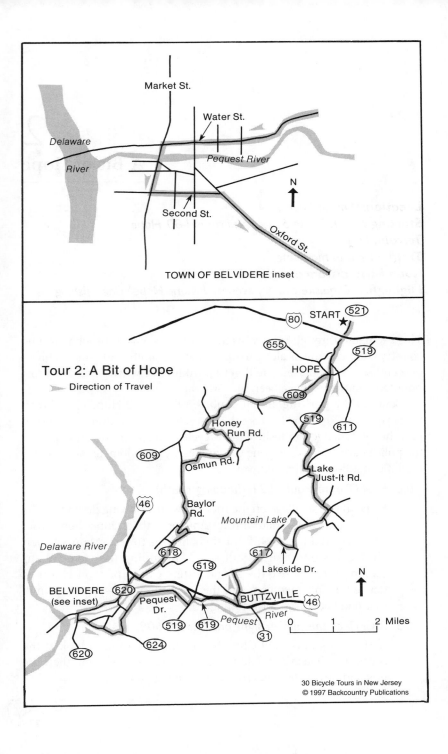

Market St.

Water St.

Delaware

Pequest River

River

N

Second St.

Oxford St.

TOWN OF BELVIDERE inset

80 START 521

655

519

Tour 2: A Bit of Hope

HOPE

Direction of Travel

609

519

611

Honey
Run Rd.

519

609

Osmun Rd.

Lake
Just-It Rd.

46

Baylor
Rd.

Mountain Lake

Delaware River

618

617

519

Lakeside Dr.

BELVIDERE
(see inset)

620

BUTTZVILLE 46

Pequest
Dr.

519

0   1   2 Miles

620

519   619   *Pequest   River*

624

31

30 Bicycle Tours in New Jersey
© 1997 Backcountry Publications

4.6 LEFT onto Honey Run Road.

This narrow, wiggly, somewhat bumpy road is nearly devoid of traffic in addition to offering wonderful scenery.

5.5 RIGHT onto Osmun Road.

Bear right at the fork and be prepared for some hard work through farm country; the road goes steeply uphill for about 1.2 miles.

6.9 LEFT at the T onto (unmarked) Baylor Road.

Practically free of traffic, Baylor Road is steep at first, but shortly after a beautiful valley vista about 1 mile ahead, you'll be rewarded by a downhill section. Use caution as you come to a sharp S-curve at the foot of the hill.

8.8 RIGHT at the T on Route 618 toward Belvidere.

Cows and horses graze lazily alongside this narrow road.

10.3 RIGHT onto Route 46, then take the first LEFT onto Route 620 toward Belvidere.

Use extreme caution entering and crossing Route 46; this is a busy artery with fast-moving traffic. After about 1 mile, Route 620 undergoes a name change to Water Street as it takes you into Belvidere, the county seat, which was established in 1825. Snacks and drinks are available.

12.1 LEFT onto Market Street.

12.3 LEFT onto Second Street.

In about 0.1 mile you'll come to the town square, built in 1826. Sensational trials and hangings took place here. An attractive park is on your right and the town's impressive restored county courthouse is on your left. You may wish to stop for refreshments before exploring the area on foot or by bicycle. Three attractive churches, some municipal buildings, and several interesting older homes face the park. Robeson Mansion, at Second and Mansfield Streets, dominates the square. Built in the Federal style in 1834 by John Paterson Bryan Maxwell, it once hosted presidents, cabinet members, and important families in Warren County's history. Today it houses the Warren County Guidance Center. When you're ready to resume the tour, continue east on Second Street.

12.6 RIGHT at the T onto Oxford Street.

13.5 LEFT onto Pequest Drive.

This narrow, uphill stretch travels through farm country and grazing land.

15.8 LEFT at the T onto Route 519 and cross the bridge.

15.9 RIGHT after the bridge onto (unmarked) Titman Road.

16.4 RIGHT (east) onto Route 46.

Use extreme caution on this busy highway. The sparkling, fast-flowing Pequest River, well stocked with trout, is on your right. After about 0.3 mile, you'll come to Hot Dog Johnny's, an institution for ice cream, birch beer, buttermilk, french fries, and, of course, hot dogs. This is a great spot to relax and enjoy the fabulous river view. Rest rooms and water are available. After your rest stop, continue east on Route 46.

17.0 LEFT onto Route 617 in the town of Buttzville.

You'll feel like you're on a roller coaster on this stretch as you pass horse-rental farms about 1.6 miles up the road.

19.1 RIGHT at the sign for Mountain Lake onto Lakeside Drive South

Rest rooms and food are available as you circle this small lake that's surrounded by houses. Continue straight ahead as a road from the west side of the lake joins in on the left.

20.8 LEFT onto Lake Just-It Road.

Trees and shrubs lining both sides of the road provide shade on a hot summer's day as you wind around this narrow, hilly, well-paved road. Stay left at the junction with Hissim Road.

22.9 RIGHT (north) onto Route 519.

24.4 STRAIGHT ahead at the flashing light onto what is now Route 521.

25.7 ARRIVE at the parking lot entrance on the left.

3
Allamuchy

Location: *Sussex, Warren, and Morris Counties*
Starting point: *A&P, Route 517, Andover*
Terrain: *Hilly with some steep ascents*
Traffic: *Moderate*
Round-trip distance pedaled: *44.2 miles*
Highlights: *Swimming, fishing, historic Waterloo Village, Morris Canal lock, scenic river, lakes, and ponds*

If you're here during the summer months, toss a bathing suit and towel into your saddlebag. This trip, which meanders through the hills of the Allamuchy region, passes by several lakes, affording many opportunities for swimming and fishing as well as numerous places to relax and listen to the melodious sound of water as it tumbles over rocks.

Waterloo Village is one of the highlights of this trip. Steeped in history, Waterloo was a favorite camping spot of the Lenni-Lenape tribe. In the 1830s, settlers enjoyed prosperity here after the Morris Canal was completed. An engineering miracle, the canal carried Pennsylvania anthracite to Andover Furnace and Andover Forge, the original name of the village. Now a historic site, the village has been restored to the way it looked during the early 19th century.

Start out early in the day, and avoid summer weekends when people from surrounding towns clog the roads traveling to the best swimming holes.

Park at the A&P on Route 517 in the Borough of Andover.

0.0 LEFT (north) onto Route 517.

0.1 STRAIGHT onto Route 613.

0.5 RIGHT onto Roseville Road.

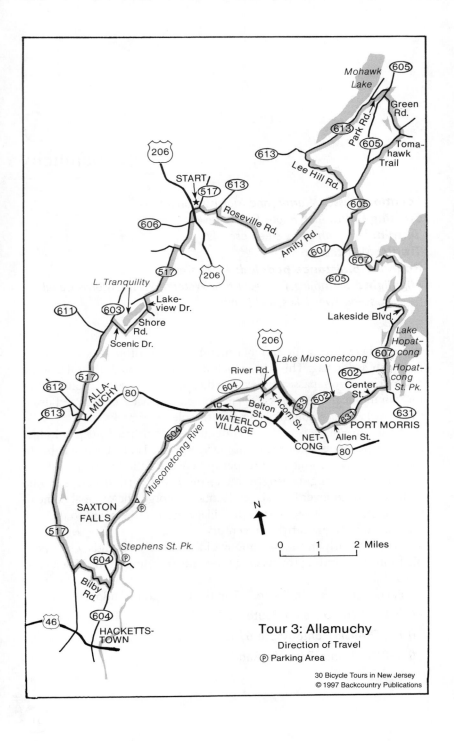

During the early-morning hours of hot summer days, you'll be shaded by a thick canopy of leaves as you pedal along this hilly, traffic-free, narrow road. Cross over the one-lane bridge at 1.5 miles, bearing left at 2.3 miles. Wolf Lake is on your right; just after the railroad overpass, Roseville Pond appears on your left. Water lilies dot the surface of the lake while daylilies and daisies grow along its bank.

3.1 LEFT onto Amity Road.

Another small pond is on the left at 4.4 miles before a steep 0.3-mile climb.

5.0 LEFT onto Lee Hill Road.

The road goes steeply uphill and keeps climbing for about 0.5 mile through a housing development. You'll soon encounter a few sharp downhill curves, then a small pond on your left.

6.6 RIGHT at the T onto Route 613, East Shore Drive.

East Shore Drive follows along the shore of Mohawk Lake, which is surrounded by an upscale community. Unfortunately, the appealing beach is private—but watching the sailboats from the road is a consolation prize. While cycling this section and admiring the pleasant views, you may feel as though you're on a roller-coaster ride.

8.8 RIGHT onto Park Road.

Take a deep breath; this section climbs uphill.

9.4 RIGHT onto Route 605.

Continue uphill.

9.5 LEFT onto Green Road.

Starting out uphill, this curving, extremely narrow road levels out in about 0.3 mile. Fortunately, it's free of traffic, and during spring and summer months you'll have lots of opportunities to examine a multitude of wildflowers growing alongside the road.

10.6 RIGHT onto Tomahawk Trail.

You may wish to stop at Tomahawk Lake Water Park at 11.3 miles, billed as "New Jersey's Longest Waterslide." (Open summer months; fee.)

Lake Hopatcong, the state's largest lake, is a great place to watch ice fishing during winter months.

11.8 **LEFT at the T onto Route 605.**

14.3 **LEFT at the stop sign onto Route 607.**

This is a sharp left turn with a steep climb for about 0.6 mile. Bear Pond is on the left at 15.1 miles. The road is quite narrow with a narrow shoulder, but there's little traffic except on summer weekends. Lake Hopatcong, which you'll be riding along for a while, is New Jersey's largest lake, with 45 miles of shoreline. Besides drawing all types of boats, the lake offers a large picnic area and a fine beach, plus iceboat races and ice fishing during winter months. There are many opportunities to purchase food and/or drinks as you go through town.

After passing the bridge that goes over one arm of the lake and marina, follow Route 607 as it turns left on Hopatcong Road (at 18.5 miles), then right on Lakeside Boulevard (at 18.7 miles).

20.0 **LEFT at the entrance to Hopatcong State Park.**

This is a great place to swim, rest, have lunch or a snack, or use the rest-room facilities. When you're finished, return to the road and pick up the mileage.

20.0 **LEFT onto Route 607.**

USE CAUTION: Traffic abounds on this four-lane, shoulderless road.

20.3 **RIGHT at the sign for Port Morris.**

This road, which becomes Center Street and then Allen Street, goes into Netcong. Lake Musconetcong, great for trout fishing, is visible at 21.7 miles.

22.6 **RIGHT at the T onto Route 183 (toward Newton).**

Here you'll have a splendid view of the length of Lake Musconetcong. Food can be purchased at 23.1 miles, just before Route 183 merges into Route 206.

24.2 **LEFT onto Acorn Street.**

Use caution crossing Route 206. After 0.1 mile, jog to the left, then right, staying on Acorn Street.

24.7 **RIGHT onto Belton Street, then RIGHT onto River Road.**

25.0 LEFT at the T onto Route 604, Waterloo Road.

You'll enter Allamuchy Mountain State Park at 25.2 miles. Riding in the woods along this smooth, lightly traveled road is very pleasant.

26.6 LEFT at the entrance to Waterloo Village.

Time seems to stand still at Waterloo Village. Here, in this tiny hamlet situated along the Musconetcong River in a valley between the Allamuchy and Schooley mountain ranges, you'll be transported back in time and catch a glimpse of what the village looked like when English settlers came in the early 1700s.

The village, a living museum designed to preserve the artifacts of our colonial roots, features working craftspeople and costumed guides. The buildings are filled with period furniture, art objects, and antiques, and the aroma of freshly ground corn from the gristmill will add to the sensation of being in another era. Before leaving, plan on visiting the Indian Village, and walk down the tree-lined path of the Morris Canal to see how the water-powered gristmill and sawmill operated. You can also pick up a free schedule of upcoming concerts held during summer months. (Hours are subject to change and season; call 973-347-0900 in advance. Fee.)

26.6 LEFT onto Route 604, Waterloo Road.

The woods and fields provide a visual treat.

29.6 LEFT into the Saxton Falls parking area (at the Morris Canal sign).

Part of Allamuchy Mountain State Park, this is the site of one of the locks of the Morris Canal, which linked Phillipsburg, Pennsylvania, with Jersey City, New Jersey. Opened in 1832, the Morris Canal was the chief means of transporting anthracite coal and iron across the state. During 1866, its most prosperous year in operation, the canal carried almost 900,000 tons of freight. Dug entirely by pick and shovel, it was the first American canal built to climb hills. By way of an ingenious series of 23 inclined planes and 34 locks, 70-ton barges were set onto giant cradles and then hauled up rail tracks by chains to water levels reaching as high as 100 feet. It took 5 days to tow boats the canal's entire length of

106 miles. The once highly successful canal was abandoned a century later when railroads proved a faster and less costly way to transport coal.

From this location you'll see the dam and one of the lock structures. Fly-fishers enjoy this spot, too.

31.2 LEFT at the entrance to Stephens State Park.

A short road leads to the park office. Stephens State Park is part of Allamuchy Mountain State Park and is a super place to relax, listen to bird calls, picnic at the edge of the Musconetcong River, take a short walk, fill up your canteen, or use the rest-room facilities.

Limestone was extensively mined here during the latter part of the 19th century, and next to the office stands a kiln used to produce lime during that period. (Open daily; free.)

31.6 TURN BACK onto the park entrance road.

Follow the one-way signs. The exit road parallels the river.

32.0 LEFT onto Route 604.

32.9 RIGHT onto Bilby Road.

Climbing uphill through a wooded area, you'll encounter housing developments that, thankfully, are well hidden behind the foliage.

33.8 RIGHT (north) onto Route 517.

Route 517 narrows to a single lane with a shoulder. (You may wish to come back another time to explore nearby attractions: the Pequest Hatchery, Deer Lake, Wild West City.) Panther Valley's shops are on the left at about 35.7 miles, and Allamuchy Lake is on the right at about 36.5 miles. Use caution at the intersection of I-80 at about 36.9 miles; usually there's heavy traffic here. A hilly area lies ahead.

39.8 RIGHT on Scenic Drive.

The one-lane bridge at 40.1 miles offers a nice view of Lake Tranquillity.

40.2 LEFT onto Shore Road.

The lake is on your left.

41.0 LEFT at the T onto Lakeview Drive.

This is the eastern end of Lake Tranquillity.

41.2 RIGHT onto Route 517.

Pastoral scenes are a welcome sight, followed at 32.1 miles by the last view of water on the trip—tiny Buckmire Pond. Follow Route 517 as it turns right on Whitehall Road; then go left on Decker Pond Road. Good Shepherd Catholic Church on the right has an unusual design and an impressive bell tower. Routes 517 and 206 join in Andover; stay on Route 517 as they separate.

44.2 ARRIVE at the starting point.

4

Port Murry to Pequest Delights

Location: Warren County
Starting point: Well-Sweep Herb Farm, Mount Bethel Road, Port Murry
Terrain: Hilly
Traffic: Light
Round-trip distance pedaled: 16.9 miles
Highlights: Herb farm, trout hatchery, education center, lovely scenery

Start out early in the day for this wonderful tour, so that you'll have plenty of time to enjoy a leisurely ride through the country side with stops at two outstanding attractions—Well-Sweep Herb Farm (where the trip begins) and the Pequest Trout Hatchery and Natural Resource Education Center. Go with an Empty car trunk—you'll want lots of room to take home the fruits and vegetables for sale along the route, as well as the unusual herbs for sale at Well-Sweep. Ask permission to park.

Limber up by wandering through the self-guiding 120-acre farm. Most herbs are marked, including borage, known for its cucumber flavor and pretty star-shaped flowers used in decorating drinks and cakes; rose geranium, great in apple jelly; summer savory, delcious with beans; tansy, supposely good when dried for keeping ants away from food; and the intruging rosemary plantings in the topiary forms known as standards. There's a Knot Garden, typical of those seen in England, with 80 varieties of scented-leaf geraniums and lush lavender. You'll also find the well-sweep—a long pole with a bucket attached above a well—that the farm was named for standing in front of the house. The pole, or sweep, lowers the bucket into the water; when the bucket is filled, its weight pulls it from the water automatically—thus the term *well-sweep*.

At Pequest Trout Hatchery and Natural Resource Center, stretch your

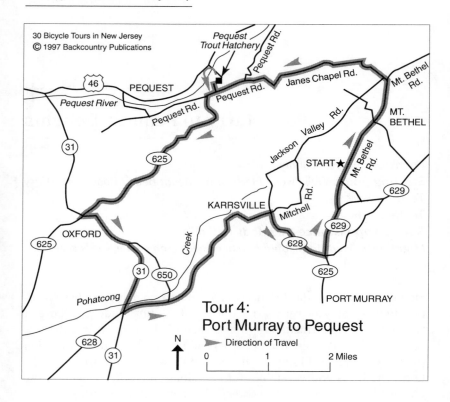

legs along short, easy nature trails; take a self-guiding tour of the trout hatchery, where approximately 600,000 brown, rainbow, and brook trout are raised each year to stock more than 200 of New Jersey's lakes, streams, reservoirs, and rivers; view *Hooked on Nature,* a 16-minute video describing how eggs are taken from the hatchery's own brood stock, and how brooks and streams are stocked with the fish raised here; and enjoy the many hands-on displays inside the beautiful exhibit hall, where you'll learn how geologists discovered the huge Pequest Valley aquifer. If you like to fish, bring a rod, have your license along, and return after your ride to catch dinner along the Pequest River, just outside the hatchery. It's one of the prettiest fishing spots in the area.

0.0 LEFT (north) onto Mount Bethel Road.

Houses along this country road, spread far apart, are almost hidden in the woodsy setting. After a 0.3-mile decline, you'll encounter gentle ups and downs for about 1 mile. Along the way, you're likely to spot squirrels, chipmunks, or an occasional red fox.

1.5   LEFT onto Janes Chapel Road.

Cycling this quiet road is a pleasure, but when the acorns start dropping, you'll be happy you're wearing a helmet! Stately weeping willows on the right side add to the lovely scenery, which is particularly impressive during fall. Don't be surprised if a deer darts out onto the road; you'll be passing densely wooded areas.

4.1   LEFT at the sign for Pequest Wildlife Management Area (Pequest Road).

4.4   RIGHT into a parking area.

I recommend taking the self-guiding tour of this trout hatchery. From the observation deck, you can see the concrete raceways used to keep trout until they're large enough to be released. Between 3000 and 7000 gallons of water a minute flow through these raceways. According to naturalist Paul Tarlowe, the hatchery—which opened in 1982—provides ideal growing conditions for trout and supplies more than 250,000 licensed anglers with healthy trout each year. He encourages visitors to come and see what makes this facility one of the most modern in the nation.

When you've finished viewing the hatchery, exit from the parking lot area and turn RIGHT onto Pequest Road.

5.2   LEFT onto Route 625.

This lightly traveled country road, lined with trees and vast cornfields, is nicely shaded during summer months. USE CAUTION at 6.2 miles; a downhill section follows for 0.7 mile after a sharp curve, followed by a brief level stretch and then numerous ups and downs. You'll come to the town of Oxford at 7.4 miles and then see a campground nestled in the woods at 8.4 miles.

8.6   LEFT onto (unmarked) Route 31.

There may be a bit of traffic in this area; use the shoulder and enjoy the downhill section for about 0.5 mile. If you'd like to take a break, there's a roadside table at 9.6 miles.

10.1   LEFT onto Route 628 East.

Cyrus Hyde stands in front of the old-fashioned well-sweep that the herb farm is named for.

Elegant homes line this quiet road. During summer months, you might want to stop at the vegetable stand on the left side of the road at 11.7 miles. (it's refreshing to know that there are still some trusting people around: A sign on the stand asks customers to weigh what they want and, on the honor system, pay by placing money in a box that's left out in full view.) A curvy section of road, slightly downhill, proceeds past cornfields.

The road levels out. just past 13.4 miles and at the Route 628 intersection, which curves to the right, you'll find the circa-1845 karrsville School. Continue on Route 628 East, which at this point climbs slightly for about 1 mile as it heads deep into farm country.

14.9 LEFT onto Route 629 at the sign for Mt. Bethel Road.

Another country stand awaits; depending on the season, ti's filled with flowers, vegetables, or berries.

15.9 At the Y take the right-hand fork, Mt. Bethel Road.

The surrounding woods are truly invigorating, and the lack of traffic adds to the pleasure of this stretch. just before the starting point, you'll pass a beautiful row of blue spruces on the right side of the road.

16.9 LEFT at Well-Sweep Herb Farm to the starting point.

Note: You may also reverse these directions by starting the ride at the Pequest Trout Hatchery, where there is ample parking space.

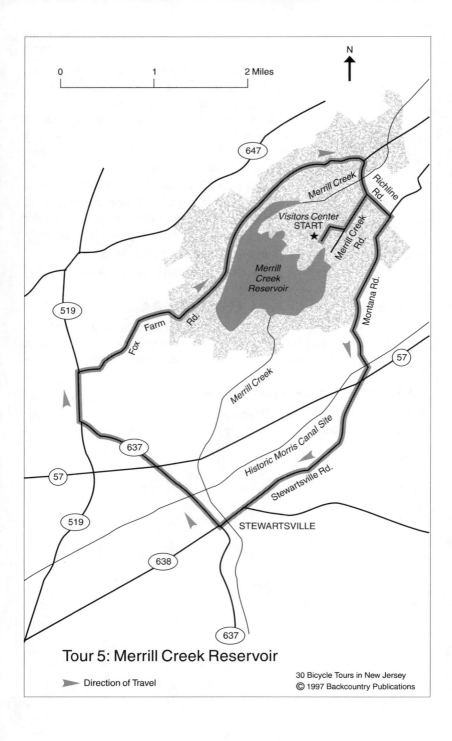

N

0   1   2 Miles

647

Merrill Creek

Richline Rd.

Visitors Center
START

Merrill Creek Rd.

Montana Rd.

519

Merrill
Creek
Reservoir

Fox Farm Rd.

Merrill Creek

57

Historic Morris Canal Site

57

637

Stewartsville Rd.

519

STEWARTSVILLE

638

637

Tour 5: Merrill Creek Reservoir

Direction of Travel

30 Bicycle Tours in New Jersey
© 1997 Backcountry Publications

5
Merrill Creek Reservoir

Location: Warren County
Starting point: Merrill Creek Reservoir, off Route 57 on Montana
  Road, Washington
Terrain: Hilly
Traffic: Light
Round-trip distance pedaled: 13.2 miles
Highlights: Merrill Creek Reservoir and Visitor Center, butterfly garden

Merrill Creek Reservoir may well be one of New Jersey's best-kept secrets. I've been back to this recreational area time and time again for the awesome views and enjoyable ride.

Before starting out, stop in at the posh, modern visitors center (open daily except major holidays 9–5; free). Besides an opportunity to fill your water bottle or use the rest rooms, you'll learn through excellent displays how this 650-acre holding area for billions of gallons of water was created atop Scott's Mountain, how water to fill the reservoir is pumped from the Delaware River during times when the river flow is high, how it's carried uphill through a 3.5-mile-long pipeline, and how the water is released to surrounding towns when the river is low and a drought has been declared.

Feel free to use the supplied binoculars or telescope to view this lovely reservoir and a bit of the surrounding 2000 acres of forest, plus a few of the birds that frequent the area. The last time I visited, a wild turkey was prancing around the side of the building! During fall and winter, there's usually a roaring fire blazing in the visitors center's stone fireplace that's very inviting for warming up before or after the ride. If you're like me, you'll return again and again for another ride or to hike one of the many trails that meander through dense woods and open fields.

The modern visitors center at Merrill Creek is a great place to relax as well as to learn how the billions of gallons of water stored in this beautiful reservoir are used.

Parking is available outside the visitors center, which is located off Route 57 on Montana Road in Washington; free, 908-454-1213.

0.0 *EXIT from the parking lot on the entrance road, and then turn LEFT onto Merrill Creek Road.*

0.6 *RIGHT onto Richline Road.*

This smooth, downhill road meanders past farms, silos, and cows.

0.9 *RIGHT at the stop sign onto Montana Road.*

The road heads uphill for a short time past open fields, followed by a nice downhill, curvy stretch. Quail and turkeys frequent this area, and in about 2 miles you'll come to a brook and bridge. The road then levels out for a very short distance before proceeding downhill again.

3.0 *RIGHT onto Route 57; take a quick jog across the road onto Stewartsville Road.*

A restaurant at this point is a reminder that civilization is near. As

Stewartsville Road continues up and down past country homes and farms, beautiful vistas can be seen, while grassy fields seem to envelop you. After an uphill stretch of about 1.7 miles, catch your breath cruising downhill through Stewartsville, a quaint town with houses bordering both sides of the road.

5.3 RIGHT at the blinker onto Route 637.

Two pretty churches, more farms, and opportunities for food and drink are ahead, as is the Morris Canal. When completed in 1833, the canal was hailed as one of the greatest engineering accomplishments. Extending for 102 miles, it climbed and descended nearly 1700 feet from Phillipsburg on the Delaware River to Jersey City on the Hudson. Boats had to be lifted and lowered via a system of locks and 23 inclined planes designed by Robert Fulton, inventor of the first practical steamboat. A boat, resting in a cradle on wheels so that it could be raised or lowered on an inclined track, would pass over natural barriers up to 100 feet high. The canal boats were capable of carrying up to 75 tons, with cargo consisting of coal, iron ore, grain, wood, potables, bricks, and lumber.

6.3 CONTINUE STRAIGHT across Route 57.

This hilly section offers lovely scenery in addition to pretty houses and large farms.

7.2 RIGHT onto Route 519.

7.8 RIGHT onto Fox Farm Road.

This steep climb is a true challenge, but you'll be able to take a quick breather at about 9 miles. Unfortunately, another short climb is just ahead.

10.5 RIGHT past the gates.

Stop here for a few minutes and be rewarded by an outstanding view of the reservoir and surrounding farmland. A dam is to your left on the way downhill.

10.7 RIGHT onto Fox Farm Road.

Pedaling past the dam's massive retaining wall is an awesome experience, as is another view of the reservoir on the right just ahead. The road goes from a fairly level stretch to a hilly area around curves, and on a warm day the breeze you'll have while pedaling downhill toward Richline Road is delightful.

12.1 RIGHT onto Richline Road at the sign for Merrill Creek.

This wooded section awakens all the senses.

12.6 RIGHT at the stop sign onto Merrill Creek Road.

12.9 RIGHT at the sign for Merrill Creek Reservoir.

Be alert; darting chipmunks, rabbits, and groundhogs often make an appearance here late in the day.

13.2 RIGHT into the parking lot.

6
Jockey Hollow and Loantaka

Location: Morris County
Starting point: Jockey Hollow Visitor Center, Jockey Hollow Road, Morristown
Terrain: Hilly
Traffic: Light
Round-trip distance pedaled: 25.7 miles
Highlights: Jockey Hollow, Loantaka Brook County Park, Great Swamp, nature center, bird-watching

George Washington slept in dozens of places, but his troops were probably most uncomfortable when they stayed in Morristown during the bitter winter of 1779–80. Washington chose nearby Jockey Hollow as a resting place for his starving, freezing, and nearly naked troops because the Watchung Mountains east of town provided cover from the British army, which was only 30 miles away in New York City at the time. It was also a logical place, because the local ironworks provided Washington's soldiers with the necessary equipment. Over the long harsh winter, his men had time to rest and reassemble, so that by the time spring came, the Continental Army was greatly reinforced. During this trip, you'll learn how the army survived, held together by Washington's leadership and ability, despite the crude huts soldiers occupied. At any rate, after touring Morristown National Historical Park, you'll be glad to return to the 20th century.

The trip then leads through tranquil Loantaka (pronounced *low-ON-a-ka;* the *t* is silent) Brook County Park and later follows through a portion of Great Swamp National Wildlife Refuge.

The Great Swamp was bought by the English in 1708 from the Delaware Indians for a barrel of rum, 15 kettles, four pistols, and various

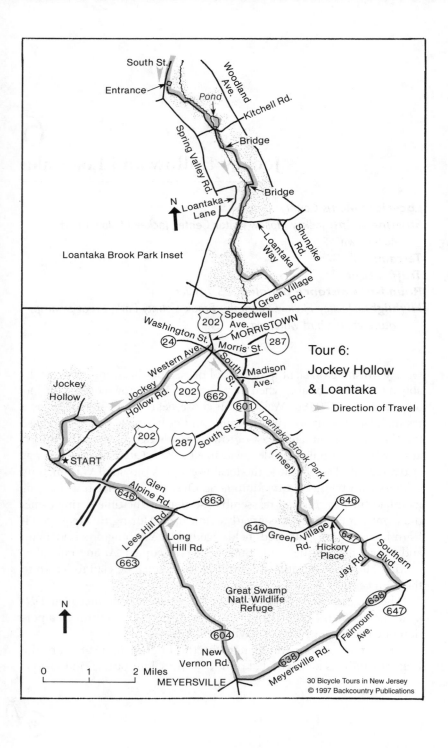

South St.

Entrance

Pond

Woodland Ave.

Kitchell Rd.

Spring Valley Rd.

Bridge

Bridge

N

Loantaka Lane

Shunpike Rd.

Loantaka Way

Loantaka Brook Park Inset

Green Village Rd.

Speedwell Ave.

202

MORRISTOWN

Washington St.

24

287

Western Ave.

Morris St.

Jockey Hollow

Jockey Hollow Rd.

202

662

Madison Ave.

South St.

601

Tour 6:
Jockey Hollow
& Loantaka

Direction of Travel

202

287

South St.

Loantaka Brook Park

(inset)

★ START

Glen Alpine Rd.

646

663

646

646

647

Southern Blvd.

Lees Hill Rd.

Long Hill Rd.

663

Green Village Rd.

Hickory Place

Jay Rd.

638

647

Great Swamp Natl. Wildlife Refuge

N

Fairmount Ave.

604

New Vernon Rd.

638

Meyersville Rd.

30 Bicycle Tours in New Jersey
© 1997 Backcountry Publications

0   1   2 Miles

MEYERSVILLE

other goods. Used for farming until the land was no longer productive, the swamp received national attention in 1959 when a jetport was proposed. Outraged citizens raised a million dollars to buy the land, which they later turned over to the Department of the Interior, and in 1968 Congress designated it part of the National Wilderness Preservation System. It is now a haven for hikers and birdwatchers as well as a variety of wildlife.

Park your car at the visitors center in the Jockey Hollow section of Morristown National Historical Park. Before starting on your trip, stop in at the center, obtain a free brochure, and spend a few minutes browsing through the displays. When you're finished, set your odometer to 0.0 at the TOUR ROAD sign at the perimeter of the parking lot.

0.0 STRAIGHT *ahead on the tour road.*

This narrow, winding road is level at first, climbing at 0.2 mile for another 0.2 mile as it passes through a forested area. Lock your bicycle at the 1.0-mile junction, and walk up to the top of the hill to see reproductions of the crude huts used by troops of the Pennsylvania line.

Yesteryear, the scene was bleak, with little to show that these 2000 men were the backbone of Washington's army. Many had marched in the 1775 invasion of Canada, fought the 1777 British crossing of Brandywine Creek, and advanced into enemy fire at Germantown.

1.0 RIGHT *onto the tour road.*

This fairly smooth road with some hills follows through a wooded area before reaching an exhibit at 1.4 miles on the left side of the road. Stop a while to read details about the life soldiers led. Military life centered on this Grand Parade area, and it was here that officers inspected troops daily. Military ceremony was as important then as it is today, and on these grounds guards were assigned, orders issued, and punishments announced.

1.6 LEFT *onto Jockey Hollow Road at the sign for Morristown.*

A rest room is immediately to the right of the turn. The road name eventually changes to Western Avenue. This section has some steep uphill climbs; the road is narrow, with no shoulder. After entering Morristown and climbing a steep 0.5 mile, you'll see a sign for Fort Nonsense at 4.5 miles. It's said that Washington had his men dig trenches and raise embankments here to give them something to do, thus its name. Although nothing remains of the fort, now commemorated by a large stone tablet, the site offers an engaging vista of the surrounding town if you have the energy for the extremely steep climb.

4.6 RIGHT onto Washington Street.

You'll pass stores and restaurants before coming to the town square, where there's heavy traffic weekdays. Impressive St. Peter's Episcopal Church is on the right at 5.0 miles. Continue straight ahead; the street name changes to South Street. Watch for Seaton Hackney Farm Park (open daily for riding; fee) on the left, and turn just after the Farm Park.

6.6 LEFT at the entrance to Loantaka Brook County Park, then an immediate RIGHT onto the bicycle path.

A nicely paved path—shared by bikers, hikers, and joggers—runs the length of this long, narrow reservation traversing fields and woods. The park is crowded on weekends but nearly empty during the week. Birds provide musical background, while deer can often be spotted in the woods.

After the duck pond in about 0.5 mile, the path goes through a parking lot and continues on the other side of a crossroad. Depending on the route you choose at the far end of the parking lot, you may have to veer slightly to the left to pick up the path again. At 8.5 miles, turn right at the bike trail junction; in a short distance you'll pass over a pretty stone bridge. Cross the next road, continuing until you reach the end of the path at Green Village Road. (The Green Village Post Office is just to your right.)

10.4 LEFT onto Green Village Road.

10.8 RIGHT onto Hickory Place.

Lovely weeping willows line this street.

11.0 RIGHT onto Southern Boulevard.

Pass the sign at the entrance to Great Swamp Outdoor Education Center. The center is a worthwhile stop, but don't take this entrance, which has a gravel road.

Loantaka Brook County Park, delightful year-round, offers easy bicycling through beautiful woods.

12.3 RIGHT onto Jay Road.

At 12.6 miles, lock your bike to a tree at the cul-de-sac and walk the dirt path that leads to the Outdoor Education Center in about 0.1 mile. This is a good place to take a break, use the rest room, fill your water bottle, and take a stretch over a bit of the 2-mile nature trail leading through woods, fields, swamps, and marshes. In addition, the center has an indoor museum with fine displays of New Jersey wildlife and natural history as well as friendly naturalists who are very knowledgeable and willing to answer questions. When you're ready to resume the tour, pick up your bike and return to Southern Boulevard via Jay Road.

12.9 RIGHT onto Southern Boulevard.

This hilly section passes through suburbs.

13.6 RIGHT onto Fairmount Avenue.

15.4 RIGHT onto Meyersville Road.

There are small hills on this stretch. Woods line the right side of the road.

17.9 RIGHT onto New Vernon Road.

You're now entering Meyersville, a good town to buy food and/or drink before reaching the Great Swamp National Wildlife Refuge. Except for the peaceful chirping of birds, the refuge is so extraordinarily quiet that even the gentle rubbing of one tree branch against another can be heard. Only an occasional airplane is a reminder that the refuge is close to the city and yet far enough away to be a home to abundant wildlife. Large oak and beech trees abound, in addition to laurel, wild orchids, and ferns.

After leaving the refuge, the road name changes to Long Hill Road, an appropriate name because of the long uphill climb.

21.8 RIGHT at the T onto Lees Hill Road.

22.2 LEFT at the traffic light onto Glen Alpine Road.

This narrow, rutted, shoulderless road is somewhat strenuous.

25.3 RIGHT at the entrance to Jockey Hollow.

25.7 ARRIVE at your starting point.

7
Skylands

Location: Passaic County
Starting point: Ringwood Manor, Ringwood State Park near the
   Sloatsburg Road entrance, Ringwood
Terrain: Hilly
Traffic: Light
Round-trip distance pedaled: 22.4 *miles*
Highlights: Ringwood Manor, Skylands Manor, Skylands Botanical
   Garden, swimming, boating, fishing

Cycling the steep hills of the Skylands area is a challenge, but the reward is definitely worth the effort. You'll be pedaling along quiet roads past tall trees, carpets of wildflowers, and beautiful bodies of water. You'll also have an opportunity to explore Ringwood State Park, which includes Ringwood Manor, the state's largest historic site, Skylands Botanical Garden, and Shepherd Lake.

The area was an iron manufacturing center from the 1700s until 1931, when the mines closed. During the Revolutionary War, everything from cannonballs to camp ovens was produced here, including the huge chain placed across the Hudson River to prevent the British from attacking West Point. The same ironworks produced the cannons for "Old Ironsides" and the mortars used by the Union Army during the Civil War.

Park in the main parking lot of the Ringwood Manor section in Ringwood State Park, not far from the Sloatsburg Road entrance. (A parking fee is charged from Memorial Day to Labor Day.) Plan on visiting Ringwood Manor, next to the parking lot, before starting out.

The discovery of iron here in 1740 led to the building of a forge and formation of the Ringwood Company. When word of this successful

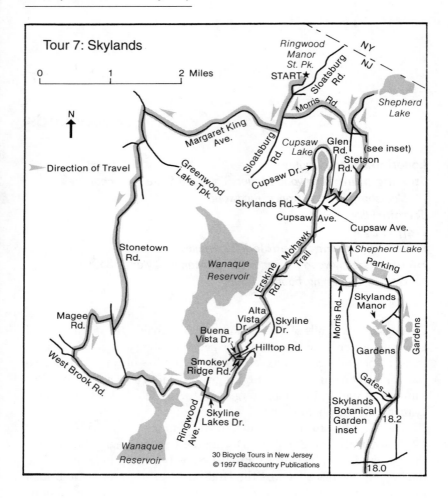

Tour 7: Skylands

0   1   2 Miles

N

Direction of Travel

Ringwood Manor St. Pk.
START

NY
NJ

Sloatsburg Rd.

Morris Rd.

Shepherd Lake

Margaret King Ave.

Sloatsburg Rd.

Cupsaw Lake

Glen Rd.

(see inset)

Stetson Rd.

Greenwood Lake Tpk.

Cupsaw Dr.

Skylands Rd.

Cupsaw Ave.

Cupsaw Ave.

Stonetown Rd.

Wanaque Reservoir

Mohawk Trail

Erskine Rd.

Magee Rd.

Alta Vista Dr.

Skyline Dr.

Buena Vista Dr.

Hilltop Rd.

West Brook Rd.

Smokey Ridge Rd.

Ringwood Ave.

Skyline Lakes Dr.

Wanaque Reservoir

30 Bicycle Tours in New Jersey
© 1997 Backcountry Publications

Shepherd Lake

Parking

Skylands Manor

Morris Rd.

Gardens

Gardens

Gates

Skylands Botanical Garden inset

18.2

18.0

operation reached England, the London Company sent its representative, Peter Hasenclever, to purchase the business and more land. After Hasenclever took over, he opened additional mines, furnaces, and forges and built the original section of Ringwood Manor in 1765.

The business, which was sold a number of times, was finally taken over by Abram S. Hewitt in 1807. In addition to continuing mining operations, Hewitt added many rooms to the mansion, which has served as headquarters for Ringwood Manor State Park since his heirs donated it to the state in 1936.

The inside of the house, filled with an eclectic collection of belongings amassed by the owners, is fascinating to explore. Outside the house are a huge Vicksburg mortar, a cannon from "Old Ironsides," and iron-making artifacts. The formal gardens behind the house are delightful; they contain an assortment of columns, gateposts, a fountain from Versailles, and imported millstones.

When you're ready to begin the bike tour, reset your odometer at the parking lot exit.

0.0 RIGHT onto the main park road, toward the park exit.

0.2 STRAIGHT onto Sloatsburg Road.

Traffic along this smooth road is usually light except during summer weekends.

0.9 RIGHT onto Margaret King Avenue.

This road is quite hilly.

3.2 LEFT at the T onto Greenwood Lake Turnpike.

A reservoir comes into view at 3.5 miles.

3.7 RIGHT onto Stonetown Road.

You'll come to a panoramic view at 4.0 miles, just before beginning a steep climb. The road winds by many distinctive houses surrounded by lush woods.

6.8 RIGHT onto Magee Road (at the Ringwood Firehouse).

Houses along this tree-lined, winding road blend in with the scenery.

8.1 LEFT at the T onto West Brook Road.

In about 1 mile follow the road as it bears right, as Stonetown Road joins from the left. At 9.2 miles you'll spot Wanaque Reservoir on the right, and as you continue along this scenic stretch, you'll have panoramic views of its clear blue water.

10.5 RIGHT at the T onto Ringwood Avenue.

10.6 LEFT onto Skyline Lakes Drive.

Food stores are available if you need supplies.

10.8 LEFT at the Y as the road divides.

One of the two Skyline lakes is on the right.

11.7 LEFT onto (unmarked) Smokey Ridge Road.

This is the first left turn after Mountain Glen Road; the grade is extremely steep.

11.9 RIGHT onto (unmarked) Hilltop Road.

Turn just before the DEAD END sign. Unfortunately, the steep climb continues.

12.0 RIGHT at the T onto Buena Vista Drive.

Take a deep breath and keep climbing.

12.1 LEFT onto Alta Vista Drive.

The road starts steeply uphill, but it levels off after a short distance as it curves through an attractive neighborhood and then straightens near the end.

12.9 LEFT onto Skyline Drive.

USE CAUTION: There's lots of traffic here. A shopping center is located opposite the road where you turn.

13.2 RIGHT onto Erskine Road.

You'll pass a nice sandy beach at Erskine Lake; unfortunately, it's private. You're now on Lakeview Avenue.

14.0 LEFT onto Mohawk Trail.

14.4 Bear LEFT onto Cupsaw Avenue.

Cross Skylands Road at 14.9 miles; if you wish, stop at the market on the left for a cup of coffee, soda, or ice cream.

14.9 LEFT at the T at the south end of Cupsaw Lake.

15.0 RIGHT onto Cupsaw Drive.

This road follows the lake clockwise past several log cabins, log garages, and houses built with stone foundations and log walls. The houses blend in nicely with the rustic surroundings, and the weeping willows that dip gracefully into the lake add to the pleasant scene. As you travel south along the east side of the lake, you'll have occasional glimpses of boating and swimming activities during summer months.

16.9 Sharp LEFT onto Glen Road.

This is a short but steep uphill.

17.0 RIGHT onto Stetson Road.

17.1 LEFT at the intersection with Skylands Road.

As you pass through the stone entrance gate into Ringwood State Park in 0.1 mile, you might like to rinse your face with the cool water from the brook that flows under the road.

17.3 RIGHT at the T onto the unmarked park road.

Follow this paved road as it hooks to the left in a semicircle. Tall trees line both sides of the road leading you to Duck Pond on the left at 17.5 miles. Resembling a Japanese garden, this tranquil spot has large white rocks jutting through the pond's surface and a beach in case you'd like to relax and listen to the birds.

18.0 Bear RIGHT at the T.

18.2 Bear RIGHT, then LEFT at the T.

Supported by huge stone pillars, these massive iron gates sport the seal of the state of New Jersey. At 18.3 miles, park and lock your bicycle and walk to the left to explore Skylands Manor and its grounds.

Amassed by Francis Lynde Stetson in the mid-1800s from surrounding pioneer farmsteads, this land was named Skylands Farms. Stetson built an impressive mansion and maintained a working farm, entertaining such friends as Grover Cleveland, Andrew Carnegie, Ethel Barrymore, and J.P. Morgan. When Clarence McKenzie Lewis bought the property in 1922, he immediately set out to make it a botanical showplace, tearing down the Stetson mansion and erecting his own Jacobean mansion of native granite. He collected and planted trees from all over the world as well as from New Jersey roadsides, and today Skylands has one of the finest collections of plants in the state. It was designated the state's official botanic garden in 1984.

After touring the manor, return to the road, cross to the other side, and visit several small gardens.

When you've finished looking at the gardens, return to your bicycle, continuing on the same road.

Ringwood Manor, within Ringwood State Park, is an impressive mansion. Take a tour and see the wealth of items amassed by the many families who lived there, and then stroll through the gardens.

The formal annual garden ahead, on the right, has seasonal exhibits. At 18.4 miles, you'll see one of the state's fanciest comfort stations, made of stone. Just after that, as the road swings left, you'll pass a stone pump house.

Take the middle fork when the road divides after passing a parking lot.

18.6 RIGHT onto the road to Shepherd Lake.

Dense woods border the road; in about 0.75 mile, you'll enter a stone and iron gate into the Shepherd Lake section of Ringwood State Park. Turn right to see the boating area and a lovely view of the lake. In season, you'll see a number of canoes and sailboats, and if you have the urge to exercise your arms, rent a canoe or rowboat.

Turn around and head in the opposite direction toward the swimming area, where you'll find rest rooms, a snack bar (in season), and a changing house. This is a beautiful place to enjoy a swim. When you're ready to continue, return to the entrance gate and head back on the park road.

20.4 Bear RIGHT at the stop sign, then RIGHT onto Morris Avenue.

If you glance to your left before turning, you'll see a pair of stone eagles guarding this entrance to the Skylands area.

21.8 RIGHT onto Sloatsburg Road.

22.1 Bear LEFT into the Ringwood Manor section of Ringwood State Park.

22.4 ARRIVE at the starting point.

8

Bergen's Northwest Corner

Location: Bergen County
Starting point: James A. McFaul Environmental Center, Crescent
  Avenue, Wyckoff
Terrain: Moderately hilly
Traffic: Moderate
Round-trip distance pedaled: 21.8 miles
Highlights: Nature center, bird-watching

One of the four original counties of New Jersey, Bergen County, created in 1683, is home to nearly 1 million people—and there are times when it seems as though every one of them is out walking or driving at the same time. However, if you allow enough time to explore the pleasant retreats built into this trip, the more highly traveled areas are tolerable.

Park at the James A. McFaul Environmental Center, where the trip begins; it's an excellent place to limber up while enjoying informative exhibits. The center's pond attracts snow geese in the fall, while ducks and turtles are a familiar sight during summer months. Interior exhibits include live frogs, toads, and an enormous Mexican tarantula, as well as samples of various bird eggs and nests. There are also garden areas and a delightful short trail to explore; you'll pass through an upland forest, streams, and a swamp area. The 81-acre Environmental Center is open daily 8:30–4:45, except on holidays; free, 201-891-5571.

Follow the one-way road out of the parking lot, and reset your odometer when you reach the exit.

0.0 RIGHT turn at the parking lot exit onto Crescent Avenue.

0.3 RIGHT onto Franklin Avenue (Route 502).

The exciting downhill portion is worth the heavy auto traffic along this section.

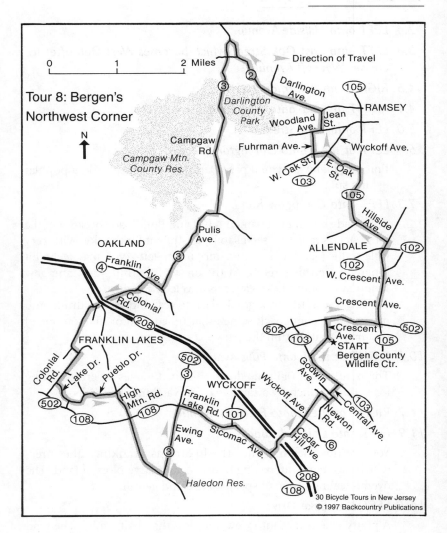

0 1 2 Miles

Tour 8: Bergen's
Northwest Corner

N

Direction of Travel

Darlington
Ave.

105

RAMSEY

Darlington
County
Park

Woodland
Ave.

Jean
St.

Campgaw
Rd.

Fuhrman Ave.→

←Wyckoff Ave.

Campgaw Mtn.
County Res.

W. Oak St.

E. Oak
St.

103

2

3

Pulis
Ave.

3

105

Hillside
Ave.

OAKLAND

Franklin Ave.

4

ALLENDALE

102

102

Colonial
Rd.

W. Crescent Ave.

208

Crescent Ave.

FRANKLIN LAKES

502

Crescent
Ave.

502

103

START
Bergen County
Wildlife Ctr.

105

Colonial
Rd.

Lake Dr.

Pueblo Dr.

502

3

Godwin
Ave.

Wyckoff Ave.

103

108

High
Mtn. Rd.

WYCKOFF

Central Ave.

108

Franklin
Lake Rd.

101

Newton
Rd.

Ewing
Ave.

Sicomac Ave.

Cedar
Hill Ave.

6

3

208

Haledon Res.

108

30 Bicycle Tours in New Jersey
© 1997 Backcountry Publications

0.9 LEFT onto Crescent Avenue, which turns into West Crescent.

The next few miles take you through the neighborhoods of Wald-
wick, Allendale, and Ramsey, which are shaded by large trees. On
weekends many yard sales are held along this route, so start out
with empty saddlebags and lots of change.

2.4 LEFT onto Hillside Avenue.

3.8 LEFT onto East Oak Street, which becomes West Oak after it crosses Wyckoff Avenue.

4.5 RIGHT onto Fuhrman Avenue.

4.9 RIGHT at the T onto Woodland Avenue.

5.0 LEFT onto Jean Street.

5.4 LEFT at the T onto Darlington Avenue.

Entering Mahwah, you'll pass Darlington County Park, a popular fishing spot.

7.3 LEFT onto Campgaw Road.

This road should be renamed "Huff and Puff Road" because of the long, steep grade that seems to head straight for the sky. With very little traffic—and a large cemetery to the left—you may feel a bit lonely along this stretch. At the crest of the hill, the Campgaw Mountain County Reservation is a welcome sight.

The reservation is a good place to rest and have a drink. You may wish to come back some other time to ski or hike on one of the many trails within the park.

10.2 RIGHT at the T onto Pulis Avenue.

The pond about 0.5 mile down this road makes a perfect setting for sitting, munching a sandwich, or watching the ducks.

11.7 RIGHT at the T onto Franklin Avenue.

11.9 LEFT onto Colonial Road.

You are now heading into the luxurious Franklin Lakes area, which has many interesting houses set on large plots of land. The overall feeling is one of spaciousness and gentility.

14.1 LEFT onto Lake Drive.

A pretty lake comes into view after less than half a mile. The road name changes to Dogwood Trail as it meanders along.

14.7 RIGHT onto Pueblo Drive.

15.1 RIGHT onto High Mountain Road.

Beautiful large houses line this street. Watch out for fast auto traffic at the circle in about 0.5 mile. Continue straight ahead.

A closer look at Canada geese at the James A. McFaul Environmental Center

16.6 LEFT onto Ewing Avenue.

Haledon Reservoir, on the right, can be seen through the trees. The Lorrimer Nature Center, run by the New Jersey Audubon Society, is about 0.9 mile down the road. This is a great place to take a break, fill the canteen, and explore.

The visitors center, built in the 1850s by Lucine L. Lorrimer, houses a classroom, observatory, museum, bookshop, and gift shop. Peer through the telescope and you'll probably see a chickadee, a cardinal, or a devious squirrel trying to steal seed from the bird feeders. A self-guided trail system meanders through the field and woodland where deer, raccoons, and rabbits are frequently spotted. Trails are open daily from dawn until dusk; the visitors center and rest rooms are open Tuesday through Saturday 9–5 and Sunday 1–5; free, 201-891-2185.

If you stop to visit the sanctuary, return to the Ewing Avenue entrance when you're ready to continue with the tour and turn LEFT, heading north.

17.6 RIGHT onto Franklin Lake Road, which becomes Sicomac Avenue.

19.3 LEFT onto Cedar Hill Avenue.

Stay left (toward Oakland) at the Oakland and Fairlawn sign and follow the road across the highway. USE EXTREME CAUTION here; watch out for fast automobile traffic.

20.6 LEFT onto Newton Road; then make the first LEFT followed by the first RIGHT onto Central Avenue.

20.8 LEFT onto Godwin Avenue.

21.4 RIGHT at the sign for the James A. McFaul Environmental Center onto Crescent Avenue.

21.8 ARRIVE at the environmental center, the end of your trip.

South Mountain

Location: Essex County
Starting point: Center for Environmental Studies, 621 Eagle Rock
Avenue, Roseland
Terrain: Very hilly
Traffic: Moderate
Round-trip distance pedaled: 26.1 miles
Highlights: Exhibition at the Center for Environmental Studies, when
open, plus glacial moraine, fishing, beautiful scenery in the South
Mountain Reservation, arts and crafts studios

If Robert Treat were still alive, he could probably sell someone the Brooklyn Bridge. Back in 1666, after leaving Connecticut with a group of Puritans to establish a new community in New Jersey, Treat purchased most of what is now Essex and Union Counties from the Lenni-Lenape tribe for a mere "50 double hands of powder, 100 bars of lead, 20 axes, 20 coats, 10 guns, 20 pistols, 10 breeches, 50 knives, 20 hoes, 850 fathoms of wampum, three troopers coats, and 32 gallons of water." The Native Americans must have been pleased, because 11 years later they sold the settlers more land, including the top of what is now South Mountain, for only "two guns, three coats, and some rum."

Essex County has changed through the years from lovely meadows and lush woodland to one of the most densely populated and industrialized counties in the state. However, it also boasts the oldest county park system in the United States and has over 5000 acres of parks, reservations, and golf courses.

If you want to get a good idea of what shape you're in, cycling up and down the hills of western Essex County is an excellent test, but plan on doing this trip on the weekend to avoid weekday rush-hour traffic. Also,

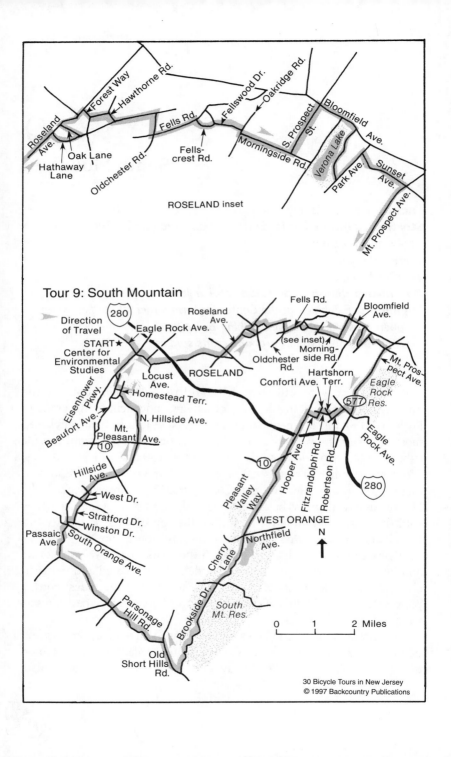

ROSELAND inset

Tour 9: South Mountain

Direction
of Travel

START ★
Center for
Environmental
Studies

ROSELAND

WEST ORANGE

South
Mt. Res.

0   1   2 Miles

30 Bicycle Tours in New Jersey
© 1997 Backcountry Publications

it's best to start out early in the morning to beat those heading over to the numerous shopping malls in the area.

Park and begin the ride at the Center for Environmental Studies at 621 Eagle Rock Avenue within West Essex Park in Roseland. If this parking lot is filled, continue to Mohawk Lane, adjacent to the center. Plan on spending a little time inside the center, but be forewarned: It may be closed temporarily due to budget cuts. When open, you can enjoy numerous exhibits ranging from dinosaur footprints found a mile away to a chart of edible mushrooms that grow in nearby parks. You can also bird-watch or limber up on a short trail in back of the center.

Reset your odometer as you exit the parking lot.

0.0 RIGHT (east) onto Eagle Rock Avenue.

Traffic is sometimes heavy along this four-lane, mostly uphill stretch through the Borough of Roseland. If you turn off to the right at Locust Avenue, you'll see the remains of the Riker Hill Quarry carved from a section of mountain. Fossilized dinosaur footprints were discovered here in 1971. You'll also see a pile of rocky debris formed about 15,000 years ago when this area was covered by the Wisconsin glacier. As the glacier receded, rocks and sand were deposited, and the smooth stones now suspended in fine soil are typical of what is called a moraine.

2.3 LEFT onto Roseland Avenue.

In the mid-1700s, stagecoaches struggled along this same road. However, unlike you, the drivers had to fight rocks, ruts, and dust.

2.9 RIGHT onto Hathaway Lane.

Numerous turn-of-the-century mansions are along this uphill stretch. Of particular interest is the Lafayette Ryerson House at 79 Hathaway Lane. Originally constructed in 1787 and moved from Wayne, New Jersey, to this location, it is built on 11 different levels, has six fireplaces, and is said to have contained slave quarters.

3.2 LEFT onto Oak Lane at the DO NOT ENTER sign.

3.4 RIGHT onto Roseland Avenue.

On the left are Tudor-style St. Peter's Episcopal Church and the stylish Essex Fells municipal offices.

3.5 RIGHT onto Forest Way; then LEFT onto Hawthorne Road.

Ride between the stone pillars and go past the school. As you pedal to the top of the hill, you'll have time to admire the thick stands of rhododendron growing on both sides of the road. During springtime, the blossoms put on a dazzling show.

4.2 RIGHT onto Oldchester Road.

No doubt your calves are beginning to feel the continuing pressure of the uphill climb. More is coming!

4.4 LEFT at the stop sign onto Fells Road.

4.7 RIGHT onto Fellscrest Road.

This is a very steep hill, but there are many attractive houses to admire while shifting gears.

4.9 RIGHT at the T onto Fellswood Drive.

At long last, the road descends—steeply.

5.2 RIGHT at the T onto (unmarked) Oakridge Road, then LEFT at the first intersection, Morningside Road.

Continuing downhill, you'll enter Verona.

5.7 LEFT onto South Prospect Street.

6.3 RIGHT onto Bloomfield Avenue.

This street has many stores, food shops, and restaurants. The attractive building on the left with a clock and cupola is Verona's Municipal Building, and to the right is Verona Park. After all the uphill work, you may want to take a break near the lovely lake and admire the weeping willow trees.

6.6 RIGHT onto the entrance road into Verona Park (at the sign).

7.0 LEFT at the T onto Park Avenue.

7.2 RIGHT onto Sunset Avenue.

Start uphill for 0.1 mile, passing a golf course on the right.

7.7 RIGHT onto Mount Prospect Avenue.

This starts out steeply but levels after 0.3 mile, followed by many ups and downs. Traffic may be heavy. At about 8.3 miles you'll come to Eagle Rock Reservation, named after the craggy cliffs once frequented by eagles. You'll know you've entered West Orange Township when you see the opulent Manor Restaurant on the right. There is usually a lot of congestion at the large shopping center at about 9.1 miles, and the going can be slow for a few minutes.

9.3 RIGHT onto Eagle Rock Avenue.

9.5 LEFT onto Robertson Road.

9.8 RIGHT at the T onto Hartshorn Terrace.

9.9 LEFT onto Fitzrandolph Road.

This road goes downhill sharply.

10.0 LEFT onto Conforti Avenue.

10.2 RIGHT at the T onto Hooper Avenue.

Attractive houses line this stretch.

10.4 LEFT onto Pleasant Valley Way.

This four-lane road has lots of traffic. Beware of grates along the curb. At 11.1 miles, there are a few stores, a gas station, and a golf course as you cross Route 10.

13.0 STRAIGHT across Northfield Avenue onto Cherry Lane.

You are now in the South Mountain Reservation. Covering 2048 acres, it is the largest of the county's reservations. Within the park lie the First and Second Watchung Mountains, Hemlock Falls, the west branch of the Rahway River, and a wide variety of flora and fauna.

After entering, you'll pass by a reservoir, lush stands of trees, fields, and picnic and play areas where there are many quiet spots to take a break or eat lunch. The numerous curves along this hilly road will keep you awake should the scenery prove too tranquil. Just before coming to Glen Avenue, the park's southern boundary, a pond comes into view at 15.9 miles.

Continue straight ahead as the road name changes to Brookside Drive, going past the Paper Mill Playhouse. Built around 1800, the playhouse was operated as a paper mill until after World War I. Today it is one of New Jersey's leading theaters.

16.3 RIGHT onto Old Short Hills Road.

As you enter Millburn Township, named for the many paper mills that once flourished in the area and the *burn,* the Scots word for "stream," the road climbs for a short stretch past large, beautiful houses.

Riker Hill Art Park, a converted Nike missile tracking station, has artists' studios and outdoor sculpture.

17.1 LEFT onto Parsonage Hill Road.

There's lots of foliage along this curving, hilly (mostly uphill), wide, lightly used road. Another park comes into view at 18.3 miles, just before a Presbyterian church, founded in 1831, on the right. Deer are frequently spotted in the wooded area ahead.

19.8 RIGHT onto Passaic Avenue.

This wide, single-lane street is usually busy with traffic. At 20.5 miles there is a large shopping center, in case you need supplies. Continue straight ahead to the first street past South Orange Avenue, which is a major intersection.

20.6 RIGHT onto Winston Drive, then LEFT onto Stratford Drive.

As you make the turn, glance over to the right to see an unusual all-white, Spanish-style house. It's one of many architectural styles found in this section.

21.2 Bear LEFT at the Y onto West Drive.

21.4 RIGHT at the stop sign onto (unmarked) Hillside Avenue.

True to its name, you'll climb uphill here as the road winds. Small, alpine-style houses are on the left at 21.9 miles. (West Essex Hospital is straight ahead if the hills have proved too much for you.) Otherwise, continue on as the road name changes to North Hillside just after it crosses Mt. Pleasant Avenue. At 23.7 miles, a crest affords a view to the west.

24.0 RIGHT onto Homestead Terrace, then an immediate RIGHT.

Riker Hill Art Park is about 0.1 mile ahead. This area, once a Nike missile tracking station, has been converted to studios for artists and craftspeople. If you take the left fork, you'll come to the potters' studios, a good place to stop and chat with the artists for a few minutes when the building is open. The artisans are friendly and willing to explain what they're doing; there's also a geological museum here, open weekdays only. When you're ready to move on, leave by the same road you entered on. Then continue straight ahead, past Homestead Terrace.

24.6 RIGHT at the T onto Beaufort Avenue.

24.9 LEFT at the end of the street; then RIGHT onto Eisenhower Parkway.

25.6 LEFT onto Eagle Rock Avenue.

26.1 ARRIVE at the starting point.

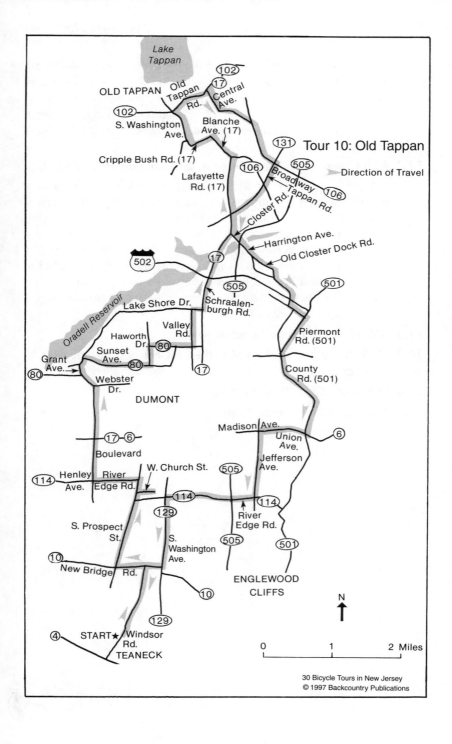

Lake Tappan

OLD TAPPAN

Old Tappan Rd.

102

17

Central Ave.

102

S. Washington Ave.

Blanche Ave. (17)

Cripple Bush Rd. (17)

Lafayette Rd. (17)

131

Tour 10: Old Tappan

106

505

Broadway

106

Direction of Travel

Closter Rd.

Tappan Rd.

Harrington Ave.

Old Closter Dock Rd.

502

17

505

501

Lake Shore Dr.

Schraalen-burgh Rd.

Oradell Reservoir

Valley Rd.

Haworth Dr.

80

Piermont Rd. (501)

Sunset Ave.

Grant Ave.

80

80

Webster Dr.

17

County Rd. (501)

DUMONT

Madison Ave.

6

Union Ave.

17 6

Jefferson Ave.

Boulevard

River Edge Rd.

W. Church St.

505

114

Henley Ave.

114

114

129

River Edge Rd.

S. Prospect St.

S. Washington Ave.

505

501

10

New Bridge Rd.

ENGLEWOOD CLIFFS

10

N

129

4

START ★ Windsor Rd.

TEANECK

0   1   2 Miles

30 Bicycle Tours in New Jersey
© 1997 Backcountry Publications

Old Tappan

Location: Bergen County
Starting point: Benjamin Franklin Junior High School, Windsor Road, Teaneck
Terrain: Mostly flat
Traffic: Light to moderate
Round-trip distance pedaled: 23.7 miles
Highlights: Historic churches, gravestone rubbing, interesting architecture, fishing

Where there's a will, there definitely is a way, and over 30 years ago our friends Laura and Marvin Mausner found it. After deciding that having young children wouldn't stop them from enjoying their bicycling, they had only one problem: Rear bicycle seats for children weren't around back then! Luckily, Marvin was ingenious; he simply cut the legs off his kitchen chairs, fastened the seats to the back fender, and off they rode. When the children grew too heavy, Marvin came up with another solution: He got them their own bikes.

Laura and Marvin shared these memories, inviting my husband and me to join them on the same route through Bergen County that they rode with their children ages ago. Amazingly, Marvin hung on to the 3-speed bicycle that once carried his son, and it took him on trips throughout the United States and parts of Europe until 1996, when he finally parted with his relic—replacing it with a secondhand 10-speed. Laura, on the other hand, decided to buy a brand-new 18-speed hybrid.

Bergen County, located in the northeastern corner of New Jersey, has a rich past. Created in 1683, Bergen is one of the four original counties of New Jersey; its first settlers were chiefly Dutch along with some French Huguenots. Because of its strategic location on the Hudson River

proximity to New York City, Bergen County played an important
uring the Revolutionary War.
Along this tour, you'll pass old churches, several small parks, and fine
_xamples of Dutch red sandstone houses. Come on a weekend not only
to avoid rush-hour traffic but also for an opportunity to pick up inexpensive merchandise at the many garage sales along the route.

Park at the parking lot of Benjamin Franklin Junior High School on
Windsor Road, just north of the Route 4 overpass. Set your odometer to
0.0 at the parking lot exit.

0.0   LEFT (north) onto Windsor Road's bike lane.

This is a quiet residential section and leads past Windsor Park at
0.2 mile. We took this trip during early-morning hours on a hot,
humid, summer day and enjoyed the shade provided by large trees
on the side of the road.

1.1   LEFT (west) at the traffic light onto New Bridge Road.

Veterans Memorial Park, which has tennis courts and other facilities open to the public, is on the right.

1.5   RIGHT (north) onto South Prospect (at the sign for Dumont).

2.6   RIGHT onto West Church Street.

Old South Church, on the left, was organized in 1723 as the
Schraalenburgh Dutch Reform Church; the original building was
erected in 1728 just 150 feet to the east of its present location. The
church became Presbyterian in 1913. Many Revolutionary War
soldiers are buried in the churchyard.

A bit farther up the street is Cooper's Pond, a lovely small park
with a duck pond. Here you can take a break in the shade of the
pagoda; watch the ducks, seagulls, and geese; and admire the
lovely spring, summer, and fall flowers. The park path takes only
a few minutes to cycle.

**3.0   RIGHT onto West Church Street. Return to Prospect Avenue
        and make a RIGHT turn, continuing north.**

3.2   LEFT onto River Edge Road, which changes to Henley Avenue.

This street goes uphill for a short distance.

4.0   RIGHT onto Boulevard.

Follow Boulevard as it swings to the left at 4.5 miles, with Webster

Drive coming in on the right. The road name then changes to Grant Avenue.

5.1 RIGHT onto Sunset Avenue, following signs to Dumont.

The Oradell Reservoir is on your left as you turn. If you're interested in fishing (permit required) or stopping for a snack along the reservoir, take Lake Shore Drive (go straight ahead instead of turning right) for a short distance as it follows the edge of the reservoir.

Sunset Avenue has many large, lovely houses and an expansive country club.

6.1 LEFT at the sign for County Route 80 (Haworth Drive).

6.4 RIGHT, still following Route 80.

Some of the houses here are in Tudor style with stone facades. After about 0.5 mile along this road, you'll come to a park with a small duck pond and benches.

7.1 LEFT at the traffic light onto Valley Road.

7.6 RIGHT at the T, then an immediate LEFT at the traffic light onto Schraalenburgh Road (County Route 17, which is also Route 39 at this location).

At 8.5 miles, cross the bridge over the Oradell Reservoir.

8.9 Bear LEFT as Closter Road comes in from the right.

Stay on Route 17, which changes names and directions several times as it winds through wooded and residential areas. At 10.0 miles, you'll come to Pond Side Park, about halfway along the route and a good spot for lunch. Approaching the center of the town of Old Tappan, you'll be on South Washington Avenue.

11.3 RIGHT onto Old Tappan Road.

As soon as you turn, you'll see the Old Tappan Sunday School, a fine example of vernacular stick-style architecture. Founded in 1883, it was the first ecclesiastical building in Old Tappan and the only place of worship in town until the 1950s. Continuing through the town, which was settled in 1682, you'll pass Trinity Reformed Church and several municipal buildings.

11.8 RIGHT onto Central Avenue.

Central Avenue runs into Broadway and proceeds through the town of Norwood. If you need supplies, a shopping center is to your left. After you pass the mall, you'll see local schools and several wooded areas.

13.4 RIGHT onto Tappan Road.

At approximately 13.7 miles, at the corner of Blanche Avenue, slow down for a look at the Campbell-Blanche House to your left. This stone house is believed to have been erected around 1790. The "Old Burying Ground" is 0.7 mile farther down the road and worth a look. Stairs and handrails have been built into the hillside as an aid in reaching the site, which is hidden from view. Over 40 headstones with single or multiple arches can be seen here; the burial ground, known as the Blauvelt Cemetery, has historical significance since it contains the graves of early settlers in Harrington Park who fought in the American Revolution; the earliest burial dates from 1722.

14.5 LEFT onto County Route 17 South.

14.6 LEFT onto Closter Road.

This is not a sharp turn. The main road (Route 17) swings to the right as you bear left heading for the center of Closter. Two cycle shops are on the left side. The street name has become Harrington Avenue and soon changes to Old Closter Dock Road. Stick with it as it turns sharply to the left at 16.0 miles.

16.3 RIGHT onto County Route 501 at the dead end after a shopping mall.

Stay on this road; as it twists along, its name changes to County Road. Canada geese flock at the small local park on the right at 17.1 miles.

18.3 RIGHT onto Union Avenue.

A few blocks south of this corner is Huyler's Landing Road. During colonial times, a crude road connected this area with the Hudson River. Cornwallis used it to attack Fort Lee in 1776, and it was also useful to the Tories when they traveled it in 1779 to raid local houses. After George Huyler improved the road in 1840, it became a major route for farm produce transported to New York until the railroad was built in 1859.

Cross the railroad tracks and turn LEFT onto Madison Avenue.

18.9 LEFT onto Jefferson Avenue at the traffic light.

After 0.7 mile, you'll see the Christie-Parsels House at 195 Jefferson Avenue, another good example of an early stone house with a gabled roof. One wing of this house dates to 1804 and the main structure to 1836. It stands on land purchased by William Christie for five pounds sterling per acre.

20.0 RIGHT onto River Edge Road.

A small park is on the left corner. River Edge Road becomes East Main Street in Bergenfield.

21.3 LEFT onto South Washington Avenue.

USE CAUTION: Traffic can be heavy here.

22.3 RIGHT onto New Bridge Road.

22.6 LEFT onto Windsor Road.

23.7 ARRIVE at the school parking lot, your final destination.

CENTRAL NEW JERSEY

11
Clinton

Location: *Hunterdon County*
Starting point: *A&P parking lot, Route 173, Clinton*
Terrain: *Hilly*
Traffic: *Light*
Round-trip distance pedaled: *40.3 miles*
Highlights: *Hunterdon Historical Museum Village, Volendam Windmill, historic buildings, country scenery, gravestone rubbing*

Clinton, a peaceful and picturesque 18th-century village, is the perfect starting point for this excursion into the hills of northwest Hunterdon County. Plan on arriving early in the morning to explore the Hunterdon Historical Museum Village, the Hunterdon Art Center, and an authentic model of a wind-driven mill. While this trip is somewhat strenuous, you'll be rewarded by dramatic panoramic vistas of well-kept farms and woods and attractive houses inhabited by people who shun city crowds. Many crisscrossing roads may be taken to shorten the trip, if you wish.

Park at the A&P shopping center on Route 173 (formerly Old Route 22) in Clinton. Take the parking lot exit opposite the Clinton Rescue Squad, resetting your odometer at the street junction.

0.0 RIGHT onto Old Route 22.

0.4 RIGHT onto Main Street.

The entrance to the Hunterdon Historical Museum Village is 0.1 mile along Main Street. Here, nestled between vertical limestone cliffs and the South Branch of the Raritan River, stands a mill built around 1810 by Ralph Hunt. Notable to historians as the only known example of a 19th-century talc mill surviving in the United States, it was first used by the Hunts to grind flaxseed to make linseed oil. People flocked to this area after the mill was built, and the town that sprang up was named, appropriately enough, Hunt's Mills. Later, to honor Governor De Witt Clinton of New York, the town's name was changed to Clinton.

First used for carding, spinning, and weaving wool and wool products, the mill—which changed hands many times through the years—was also used for manufacturing grist, talc, and graphite. Everything changed when the Mulligans became its new owners in 1857; they began quarrying the surrounding cliffs and installed kilns, a stone crusher, and a screen house to aid in the manufacture of limestone, which local farmers used for fertilizer.

Limber up by taking a short stroll through the village (open April 1 through October 31, Tuesday through Sunday 9–4; fee). You'll pass many structures, including the remains of the crusher, the general store, schoolhouse, log cabin, and a lovely herb garden overlooking the South Branch of the Raritan River and dam, where fly-fishing is very popular.

When you're ready to resume the tour, return to Main Street.

0.5 RIGHT across the bridge over the South Branch of the Raritan River.

0.6 LEFT onto Lower Center Street.

This is the first possible left turn after crossing the bridge. The Hunterdon Art Center, housed in a large stone building on your left just after making the turn, features changing exhibits and is worth a stop. (Hours are Wednesday through Sunday 11–5 and Saturday and Sunday 1–5. Donations requested.) You may wish to walk through the center of town before continuing on Lower Center Street. The downtown area has many ornate Victorian and Greek Revival houses and public buildings, looking much the same as they did a century ago.

0.7 RIGHT onto Leigh Street.

This pretty street, which becomes Hamden Road after leaving Clinton, has several small hills.

2.3 RIGHT at the unmarked intersection onto Hamden Road.

This turn, easy to miss, comes after Kent Court and continues on an older road that used to be the main drag before new housing

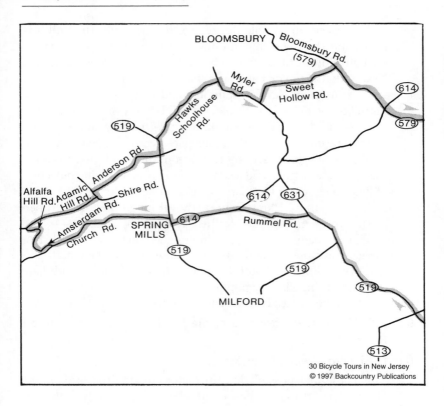

30 Bicycle Tours in New Jersey
© 1997 Backcountry Publications

developments were built. Cross the narrow steel bridge over the South Branch at 2.5 miles.

2.8 RIGHT onto Lower Landsdown Road.

3.2 LEFT onto Landsdown Road.

Tall trees shading this narrow road provide camouflage for birds, which nevertheless make their presence known by their loud chirping.

4.0 LEFT onto Sidney Road, then RIGHT onto Lower Kingtown Road.

Cross Capoolong Creek, which parallels the road a couple of times. This is a fairly steep but short uphill section. The stone house and red barns you'll pass blend in nicely with their surroundings.

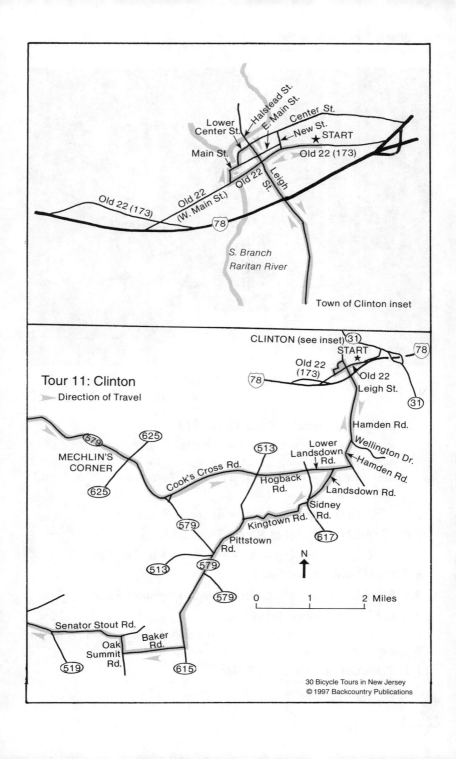

Town of Clinton inset

CLINTON (see inset)

START

Old 22 (173)

Old 22

Leigh St.

Hamden Rd.

Wellington Dr.

Lower Landsdown Rd.

Hamden Rd.

Landsdown Rd.

Tour 11: Clinton

Direction of Travel

MECHLIN'S CORNER

Cook's Cross Rd.

Hogback Rd.

Kingtown Rd.

Sidney Rd.

Pittstown Rd.

N

0   1   2 Miles

Senator Stout Rd.

Oak Summit Rd.

Baker Rd.

Halstead St.
E. Main St.
Center St.
Lower Center St.
New St.
START
Main St.
Old 22 (173)
Old 22 (W. Main St.)
Old 22 (173)
Leigh St.
S. Branch Raritan River

30 Bicycle Tours in New Jersey
© 1997 Backcountry Publications

The mill at Hunterdon Historical Museum Village

5.5 LEFT onto Pittstown Road, Route 513.

Pittstown was a natural choice for settlers because its location along the Capoolong Creek made it ideal for building a dam and mill. In less than 1 mile you'll be able to purchase food and drink and recover from the uphill stretch.

6.5 STRAIGHT onto what is now Route 579.

6.8 STRAIGHT onto what is now Route 615.

After a pond you'll come to a scenic valley and orchards.

8.3 RIGHT onto Baker Road.

9.5 RIGHT at the T onto (unmarked) Oak Summit Road.

9.8 LEFT onto Senator Stout Road.

So many cornfields crop up in this area that some cyclists might call this a "corny" trip.

11.1 STRAIGHT on Route 519 North.

The panoramic views of the surrounding countryside are marvelous here as you dip up and down the hills. In a couple of miles, there is an opportunity to purchase food and drink. Afterward, watch for a large cemetery on the right. Built in the 1700s and used by an English Presbyterian congregation, it was later shared by German Lutherans. Together, both congregations erected a new church in 1802 that is still in use today. If you enjoy gravestone rubbing, this is the place to try.

14.1 STRAIGHT onto what is now Route 631.

14.9 LEFT onto Rummel Road.

This exceptionally beautiful, hilly stretch of road through Holland Township offers breathtaking views off to the right.

16.1 Bear LEFT onto Route 614, toward Spring Mills.

This section has some of the most attractive farms along this route.

17.4 RIGHT at the stop sign onto Route 519.

17.5 LEFT onto Church Road.

19.9 RIGHT onto Amsterdam Road.

Goldfinches, designated as New Jersey's state bird, seem to favor this spot!

20.1 RIGHT onto Alfalfa Hill Road.

Wisely named and heavily endowed with trees, this road begins a steep 0.5-mile climb.

20.9 RIGHT onto Adamic Hill Road.

It's easy to think you're in Holland when arriving at the Volendam Windmill Museum, less than 1 mile up the road on your left. Lock your bicycle to the fence or a tree, eat lunch atop the hill adjoining the windmill, and take a short tour of the structure designed and built by the late Poul Jorgensen and his wife, May, in 1965. Named after the town of Volendam in the northern part of the Netherlands near Amsterdam, the museum demonstrates how a wind-driven mill is used for grinding raw grain into flour. The arms, capable of producing 40 horsepower, are sufficient to turn the 1-ton millstone within the 60-foot-high mill. Inside, you can examine old milling tools, huge gears made of applewood, wooden shoes, farm implements, and the mill's 68-foot tip-to-tip sail arms at close range. (The windmill is usually open weekends from May through September, noon–4:30, but if you call 732-955-4365 and say you're coming, a caretaker might show you around; fee.) A clean outhouse is on the grounds.

Continue on Adamic Hill Road when you've finished viewing the museum.

22.4 LEFT onto Shire Road.

22.5 RIGHT onto Anderson Road.

Beautiful blue spruces, mimosas, weeping willows, and maples adorn the local houses.

24.1 LEFT at the T onto Route 519.

Prepare for a steep uphill climb for a short distance. Rest rooms and a soda machine are available at a gas station ahead.

24.5 RIGHT onto Hawks Schoolhouse Road.

Hold on tight; the road is rough for a while but offers glimpses of beautiful views, open fields, and farms.

26.1 RIGHT at the T onto unmarked Myler Road.

To make up for all the climbs, there is a long downhill stretch, which is steep in spots. It begins to level off just before the road ends.

27.1 LEFT at the T onto Sweet Hollow Road.

Despite the houses, a feeling of solitude prevails here among the tall trees. Now you have to pay the price for coasting down Myler Road; this is mostly uphill, getting steeper as you go.

28.8 RIGHT at the T onto Route 579.

Hardly any traffic mars the beautiful views along this stretch of road. In less than 1 mile you'll begin a steep descent, but the breeze whistling through your helmet is short-lived because the next hill is within sight.

You'll pass a vineyard, apple orchards, acres and acres of corn, and a "pick-your-own" raspberry patch (in season). Spruce Run Reservoir is to the left at 32.3 miles, and at 33.2 miles you'll come to Mechlin's Corner Tavern, built in 1752. The most popular drink in the tavern was probably Hunterdon apple brandy made from homegrown apples, since every landowner in the area during the 19th century was required to plant one apple tree for each acre of owned land. After this, you'll pass through more woods and corn-fields.

34.2   LEFT onto Cook's Cross Road.

There is no shoulder on this bumpy road. Usually farmers can be seen working in these fields. The road name changes to Hogback Road and then to Lower Landsdown Road. You'll cross a beautiful one-lane bridge at 37.4 miles.

38.0   LEFT onto Hamden Road.

38.5   LEFT at the T, onto a continuation of Hamden Road.

40.0   RIGHT onto Route 173 in Clinton.

40.3   ARRIVE at the starting point.

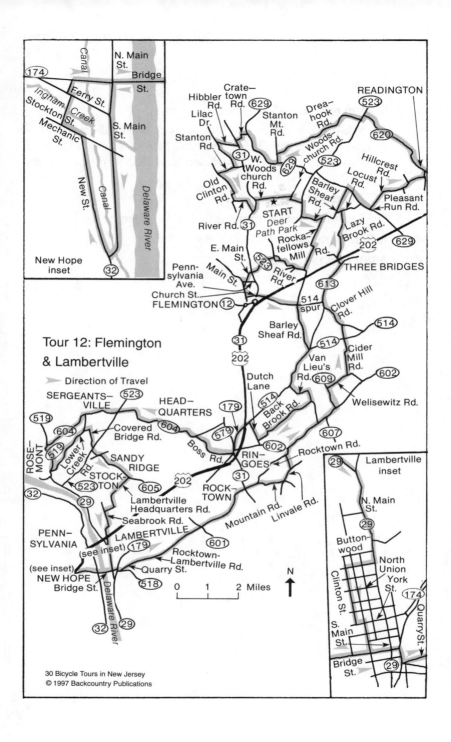

New Hope inset

174

Canal

Ingham Creek

Ferry St.

Stockton St.

Mechanic St.

New St.

Canal

N. Main St.

Bridge St.

S. Main St.

Delaware River

32

Crate—town Rd.

Hibbler Rd.

629

Stanton Mt. Rd.

Drea—hook Rd.

READINGTON

523

Lilac Dr.

Woods—church Rd.

620

Stanton Rd.

31

W. Woods church Rd.

629

523

Hillcrest Rd.

Locust Rd.

Old Clinton Rd.

Barley Sheaf Rd.

Pleasant Run Rd.

River Rd. 31

START

Deer Path Park

Rocka—fellows Mill Rd.

Lazy Brook Rd.

202

629

E. Main St.

523

River Rd.

THREE BRIDGES

Penn—sylvania Ave.

Main St.

613

514 spur

Clover Hill Rd.

Church St.

FLEMINGTON 12

Barley Sheaf Rd.

514

Tour 12: Flemington & Lambertville

31

202

514

Cider Mill Rd.

Van Lieu's Rd.

609

602

Direction of Travel

Dutch Lane

Welisewitz Rd.

SERGEANTS—VILLE

523

HEAD—QUARTERS

179

514

Back Brook Rd.

519

604

604

579

607

Covered Bridge Rd.

Boss Rd.

602

Rocktown Rd.

519

519

Lower Creek Rd.

SANDY RIDGE

RIN—GOES

Lambertville inset

29

ROSE—MONT

STOCK—TON

523

605

202

31

ROCK—TOWN

N. Main St.

32

29

Lambertville Headquarters Rd.

Button—wood

29

Seabrook Rd.

Mountain Rd.

Linvale Rd.

PENN—SYLVANIA

LAMBERTVILLE (see inset)

179

601

North Union York St.

Clinton St.

(see inset)

NEW HOPE

Bridge St.

Rocktown—Lambertville Rd.

Quarry St.

518

N

0   1   2 Miles

S. Main St.

174

Quarry St.

32

29

Delaware River

Bridge St.

29

12

Flemington and Lambertville

Location: Hunterdon County
Starting point: Deer Path Park, West Woodchurch Road, near
   Flemington
Terrain: Hilly with a few steep climbs
Traffic: Light
Round-trip distance pedaled: 75.3 miles
Highlights: Historic buildings, outlet stores and antiques shops, magnifi-
   cent rural scenery, Delaware River, Delaware Canal

Hunterdon County, located in the west-central part of the state, is steeped in history and blessed with deep valleys, gentle hills, sparkling rivers, dense woods, and pastoral scenery. It is also one of New Jersey's leading agricultural counties. This route passes many dairy and horse farms as well as numerous historic sites in towns and villages dating back to pre-Revolutionary days.

This 2-day tour begins a short distance from Flemington, which has served as the county seat since 1791 and is now one of the largest outlet centers in the state. Flemington gained national fame in 1935 when Bruno Richard Hauptmann was tried here and found guilty of kidnapping and murdering the Lindbergh baby. The courthouse is still here, as are many of the interesting Victorian structures.

Although housing developments are springing up throughout Hunterdon County, the countryside still provides one tranquil scene after another, with cows and horses grazing lazily in the fields alongside roads relatively free of traffic.

Along this route you'll pedal through New Hope, Pennsylvania, once described by William Penn as "the most beautiful of landscapes." You'll also catch a glimpse of Revolutionary-era cottages, artists' workshops, tiny gardens, and have an opportunity to ride a mule-drawn barge that carried coal along the canal over 150 years ago.

Plan on staying overnight in Lambertville or New Hope, just across the Delaware River. (Write to: South Hunterdon Chamber of Commerce, 4 South Union Street, Lambertville, NJ 08530, or Bucks County Tourist Commission, 152 Swamp Road, Doylestown, PA 18901, for information on hotels and motels. Some accommodations require a 2-day minimum stay on weekends.)

Park and begin at Deer Path Park on West Woodschurch Road off Route 31, north of Flemington. Fishing and picnicking are popular activities in this park, and swimming is available at the YMCA located on the grounds. (The pool is open daily 5:45 AM–10 PM; fee.) A parking lot is located outside the YMCA; another one is at the end of the paved road.

Reset your odometer to 0.0 at the exit from the park at the junction with West Woodschurch Road.

0.0 RIGHT onto West Woodschurch Road.

Many gradual and steep climbs lie ahead after a delightful 0.4-mile downhill stretch, but the extra effort is definitely worth the perspiration. The slightly choppy road passes picturesque farms and newly built houses.

0.7 RIGHT at the T as Woodschurch Road joins in from the left.

Sprawling farms and open fields abound in this area.

1.2 RIGHT at the T onto (unmarked) Route 523.

1.8 LEFT onto Barley Sheaf Road.

If the pleasant curves along this road don't keep you awake, its choppy surface will!

2.5 RIGHT onto Rockafellows Mill Road.

The road is very narrow and bumpy, but the interesting farms, silos, and open fields make up for the discomfort. Just before the road's end, a small bridge takes you across the South Branch; enjoy this beautiful spot.

4.5 RIGHT at the T onto (unmarked) River Road.

Canada geese and mallards can usually be seen along the banks of the South Branch of the Raritan River.

4.8 RIGHT at the first road junction, continuing on River Road.

As you pedal through this area, the scenic side of the road is immediately evident: The calm river, flanked by lush farms, flows to the right, while chemical and plastic companies mar the view to the left.

5.7 LEFT (south) onto Route 523.

After crossing State Route 31, you'll enter East Main Street in Flemington. An attractive Presbyterian church built in 1791 stands opposite an impressive stone-arched gate with ornate wrought-iron adornments.

7.1 RIGHT at the traffic circle onto Pennsylvania Avenue; then an immediate LEFT onto Main Street.

A Civil War memorial, complete with cannon, occupies the center of this circle. Main Street, usually congested with shoppers on weekends, has a number of outlet stores and restaurants. You may wish to stop, browse, and perhaps fill your saddlebags with bargains. In any case, examine a few of the historic buildings along this street.

Have a drink or lunch inside the large Union Hotel, built in 1772, where cyclists are welcome; feel free to use the rest rooms. The chamber of commerce, located in the same building, offers free brochures listing nearby attractions. Opposite the hotel is the Greek Revival courthouse built in 1828, which gained worldwide attention during the trial of Bruno Hauptmann. The Doric House, at 114 Main Street, sports fine exterior wood carving; built in 1846, it is now the headquarters of the Hunterdon County Historical Society and is open for tours by appointment. Next to it is a handsome Methodist church, built of stone.

7.7 LEFT onto Church Street.

After crossing US Highway 202, traffic thins as the road widens and passes housing developments and farms.

9.5 RIGHT onto Barley Sheaf Road.

This turn takes you into a peaceful rural area.

11.3 RIGHT at the T onto Route 514 West, following the sign for Ringoes.

12.7 LEFT onto Van Lieu's Road.

Corn sways in the breeze, and in season you'll pass places where you can handpick strawberries.

13.8 RIGHT onto Back Brook Road (just before the one-lane bridge).

Housing developments have sprung up in recent years along this narrow road.

16.1 RIGHT at the T onto Dutch Lane.

This stretch begins with a short uphill climb, but stick with it; there'll be a breeze as you pedal downhill.

16.8 LEFT at the T onto Old York Road (Route 514).

USE CAUTION crossing Routes 202 and 31; as you enter the historic town of Ringoes, you'll be on Route 179, following the same path that Native Americans traveled between the Delaware and Raritan Rivers.

18.1 RIGHT onto Boss Road.

After about 0.4, mile admire the picture-postcard scene. A large maple tree stands at the perfect spot on the roadside.

19.6 LEFT at the T onto (unmarked) Route 604.

This smooth road has hardly any traffic. At 22.7 miles you'll reach shops, a restaurant, and a general store in the village of Headquarters. As you head back into farm country, you'll be going downhill for a change.

When you reach Sergeantsville at 23.8 miles, you'll pass through New Jersey's only covered bridge. There are many theories about why covered bridges were constructed. Some think it was to keep horses from rearing when passing over the water; others think it was to protect the bridge from the elements. The most charming theory is that engineers with romance in their soul built covered bridges to allow young couples a chance to stop their carriage and embrace for a moment in privacy!

After the bridge, the road goes uphill through more exquisite farm scenery.

25.6 LEFT at the T onto Route 519.

The town of Rosemont has a general store and some antiques stores. Follow Route 519 as it turns left at the sign for Stockton. At 26.3 miles you'll begin a steep descent.

At Sergeantsville you'll cycle through New Jersey's only covered bridge.

26.7 Sharp LEFT onto (unmarked) Lower Creek Road.

After a hairpin turn, you'll practically be going back in the same direction you came from. A dark, cool stretch of forest follows beside a creek on the right. Wildflowers grow profusely along both sides of the narrow road. After climbing steeply uphill and crossing the bridge, the creek will be on your left.

28.7 RIGHT onto (unmarked) Covered Bridge Road.

This extremely narrow road starts out steeply uphill.

29.5 RIGHT onto Route 523.

29.6 LEFT onto Route 605 (south).

Jog to the left, then right, at the T at 30.0 miles in Sandy Ridge. Some small hills follow through open country.

31.3 RIGHT on (unmarked) Lambertville Headquarters Road.

As you turn, you'll squeeze past a small, squarish white building very close to the road.

33.0 LEFT at the T on Seabrook Road.

Enjoy the downhill cruise.

33.9 LEFT on Route 29 just past the Route 202 overpass.

USE CAUTION: This short stretch along Route 29 north of Lambertville is a four-lane highway with lots of traffic.

Lambertville, settled in 1705, is one of the oldest communities in Hunterdon County. During colonial times, the town flourished, for not only was it a popular stop along the stagecoach route between New York and Pennsylvania, but its thriving industry also included a canning factory, brickyard, shoe factory, linen mill, and an ironworks. The town gained a place in history when Washington visited during his campaigns of 1777 and 1778. Today, Lambertville is popular for the recreational facilities it offers at the Delaware and Raritan Canal State Park as well as its numerous antiques shops. When the canal opened in 1834, Lambertville was an important stop on the feeder link since barges could carry products from here to Trenton or New Brunswick. In addition to the historic sites, there are rows of quaint houses built very close to each other during the mid-19th century. Many sport interesting roofs, turrets, and tiny porches from which residents view passersby. And as properties are slowly being restored and new shops are opening, Lambertville is once again enjoying a reputation as the place to go for a pleasant outing.

34.5 RIGHT onto Buttonwood Street.

34.7 LEFT onto (unmarked) Clinton Street.

This is the last street on which a left turn is possible.

35.0 LEFT onto York Street, then RIGHT onto North Union Street.

This street lined with restaurants, art studios, and antiques stores also has a small and interesting Civil War memorial.

35.2 RIGHT at the traffic light onto Bridge Street.

Historic Lambertville House, built in 1812 by Senator Lambert, was originally called Lambert's Inn. Continuously hosting weary travelers since its founding, it has served many famous people, among them President Andrew Johnson, General Tom Thumb, and General Grant. Next to it is Lambertville Station, consisting of a restaurant, inn, and antiques shops.

The boyhood home of James Wilson Marshall is at 60 Bridge Street (fee). When Marshall discovered gold in California in 1848, it led to the Gold Rush of 1849.

35.6 LEFT at the traffic light onto South Main Street.

New Hope is rich in history. In 1681 William Penn granted 1000 acres to an Englishman named Thomas Woolrich. Robert Heath took possession of the acreage in 1700, and later 500 acres of the original tract were sold to John Wells, recognized as the actual founder of the town. Wells operated a ferry and tavern, and in 1764 the town was named Coryell's Ferry for John Coryell, who took over as the major landowner in the area. The ferry was important to General George Washington, for it was from this bivouac site that he planned and directed the strategy that led to winning the Battle of Trenton.

Later, after Benjamin Parry built a successful mill operation here known as New Hope Mills, the town became known as New Hope. Standing on Main Street in the center of town at 35.7 miles is the Parry Mansion, where Benjamin Parry lived until his death in 1839. Ten rooms, each furnished from a different period spanning from the late 18th century to the early 20th century, can be seen. Five generations of Parrys lived here over a period of more than 200 years. (Call 215-862-5880 for hours; fee.)

New Hope has certainly changed since the days of the Lenni-Lenape. On weekends, you'll have to weave around swarms of people and dodge auto traffic since it's jammed with shoppers who hunt for good buys and unusual clothing, food, jewelry, furniture, crafts, antiques, paintings, toys, and sculpture. (Shops are open 10–5 and some evenings during summer and Christmas season.)

A short distance to the left stands the Bucks County Playhouse, the State Theatre of Pennsylvania, which was converted from the former Parry gristmill. Plays, musicals, ballets, and concerts are presented here year-round.

36.0 RIGHT onto New Street.

You may want to stop and take a ride into the past via a mule-drawn barge. As you cross under old wooden bridges and travel through the locks of the canal, which opened in 1832, you'll get a glimpse of the oaks that once sheltered George Washington's soldiers. Perhaps you'll gain a feeling for what it was like when huge boats plied this water transporting coal and other products. (Open from April to October; fee.)

36.3 LEFT at the T onto Mechanic Street.

36.4 RIGHT at the stop sign onto Stockton Street.

Cross Ingham Creek; jog left and then right.

36.5 RIGHT onto Bridge Street.

Cross the Delaware back into Lambertville.

37.0 RIGHT at the T.

37.1 LEFT at the sign for Hopewell via Route 518, then an immediate LEFT onto (unmarked) Quarry Street.

A long climb, lasting about 1.8 miles, is followed by a pleasant downhill section, then some hills. You are now on Rocktown-Lambertville Road. USE CAUTION as you cross busy Route 31; then continue straight ahead on Rocktown Road. Lush woods provide relief from the hot sun during summer.

43.0 RIGHT onto Mountain Road.

Be careful of loose rocks along this shady road.

44.0 LEFT at the stop sign onto Linvale Road.

Daylilies line the side of the road during summer months on this downhill stretch.

45.0 RIGHT at the T onto Rocktown Road.

45.2 RIGHT at the sign for Neshanic onto Route 602.

47.4 LEFT onto Route 609.

After a climb of about 0.4 mile, your reward is an excellent vista of surrounding farm country and horse farms.

48.2 RIGHT onto Welisewitz Road.

Beautiful rural vistas extend to the left.

49.1 LEFT onto Cider Mill Road.

Back Brook runs beneath the narrow bridge. It's a good spot to stop and cool off your feet or rinse your face. Watch out for sharp curves at about 0.9 mile along this road.

50.9 LEFT at the T onto Clover Hill Road.

51.8 RIGHT *at the T onto the 514 Spur.*

52.0 STRAIGHT *onto Route 613 as the 514 Spur turns off to the left.*
Cross the bridge over the South Branch into the sleepy town of Three Bridges. This is Main Street.

53.6 Bear LEFT *in accordance with the bold arrow; then cross Route 202 almost immediately.*

53.8 RIGHT *onto Lazy Brook Road.*

55.5 LEFT *at the T onto (unmarked) Locust Road.*

55.7 RIGHT *at the T onto Barley Sheaf Road.*

56.6 RIGHT *at the T onto Route 629, Pleasant Run Road.*

57.7 LEFT *onto Hillcrest Road.*

60.2 LEFT *at the T and then another LEFT at the T onto Route 620.*

63.6 LEFT *at the T onto Route 523.*

63.7 RIGHT *onto Dreahook Road.*
Woods, fields, and a few houses line this road.

67.2 LEFT *at the stop sign onto Stanton Mountain Road.*
A panoramic view is off to the right. If you need supplies, there's a general store as you turn the corner.

67.5 RIGHT *onto Route 629.*

69.0 LEFT *onto Cratetown Road.*

69.6 LEFT *onto Route 31, then RIGHT onto Hibbler Road.*
USE CAUTION: Route 31 is a main thoroughfare.

70.3 LEFT *at the T onto (unmarked) Lilac Drive.*
After you travel through a wooded area, railroad tracks appear on the right in a short distance.

71.5 RIGHT *at the T onto (unmarked) Stanton Road.*
Cross the railroad tracks, then the South Branch.

72.2 LEFT *at the T onto Old Clinton Road.*
As you admire the views on the left, don't forget to watch out for woodchucks that may be crossing the road.

73.5 LEFT *onto River Road.*
A steep downhill stretch leads to a sharp curve.

74.4 LEFT onto (unmarked) Route 31.

USE CAUTION: Even though the road isn't marked, it's recognizable by the traffic whizzing by in both directions.

74.8 RIGHT onto West Woodschurch Road.

You can rest from this steep hill very shortly; you'll arrive at the entrance to Deer Path Park at 75.3 miles.

13
Westfield and the Watchungs

Location: *Union and Somerset Counties*
Starting point: *Echo Lake County Park, Mill Lane, Springfield*
Terrain: *Moderately difficult with some steep hills*
Traffic: *Light to moderate*
Round-trip distance pedaled: *28.6 miles*
Highlights: *Miller-Cory House, nature museum*

A blend of parks, neighborhoods, and open spaces, this route passes through several towns in western Union County before climbing into the scenic Watchung Mountains.

Union County earned a reputation for its sparkling air during the 19th century, attracting vacationers who eventually established roots here. Railroads, towns, and houses quickly sprouted. Although now communities seem to hug one another and the air is no longer so pure, wise officials took pains to set aside a good deal of land for parks, golf courses, and wildlife preserves.

Following bicycle paths through these county parks takes you through a variety of affluent neighborhoods. The ride is particularly pleasant on weekends, but traffic is heavy during weekday rush hours, so plan accordingly.

Terrain is largely flat during the first section of the ride. The few hills aren't difficult, but once you cross Route 22, you'll come to the Watchung Mountains. Although these are low enough to qualify as hills rather than mountains, they are a challenge to cyclists.

Park and begin at Echo Lake County Park on Mill Lane, just west of Springfield Avenue. This 139-acre park has two lakes and offers boating, fishing, picnicking, and ice skating. Choose a place near the Springfield Avenue side and pedal to Springfield Avenue. The mileage count begins at the junction of Mill Lane and Springfield Avenue.

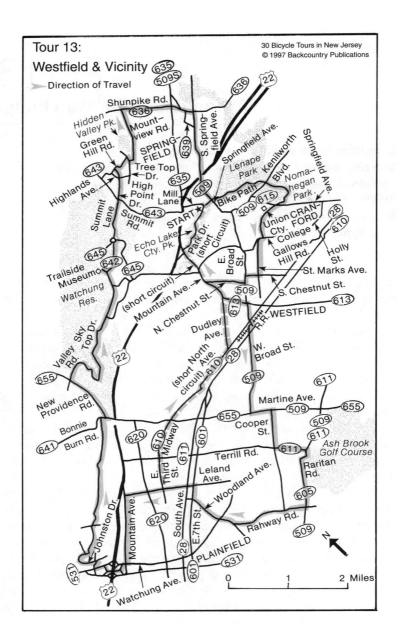

Tour 13:
Westfield & Vicinity

Direction of Travel

30 Bicycle Tours in New Jersey
© 1997 Backcountry Publications

Shunpike Rd.

Hidden
Valley Pk.

636

Mount-
view Rd.

S. Spring-
field Ave.

636

22

Green
Hill Rd.

SPRING-
FIELD

639

Springfield Ave.

Lenape
Park

Kenilworth
Blvd.

Springfield Ave.

Tree Top
Dr.

635

Noma-
hegan
Park

643

High
Point
Dr.

Mill
Lane

509

Bike Path

Highlands
Ave.

Summit
Rd.

643

START

509

615

Union CRAN-
Cty. FORD
College

28

Summit
Lane

Park Dr.
(short
Circuit)

Bike Path

Gallows
Hill Rd.

610

Echo Lake
Cty. Pk.

E.
Broad
St.

Holly
St.

645

642

645

Trailside
Museum

Watchung
Res.

(short circuit)

Mountain Ave.

N. Chestnut St.

509

513

509

S. Chestnut St.

St. Marks Ave.

613

Valley Sky
Rd. Top Dr.

22

Dudley
Ave.

R.R.WESTFIELD

655

New
Providence
Rd.

(short North Ave.
circuit)

610

28

W.
Broad St.

509

611

Bonnie
Burn Rd.

641

620

610

Midway

Third St.

601

611

655

Cooper
St.

509

655

509

611

Ash Brook
Golf Course

E.
Third
St.

Terrill Rd.

611

Leland
Ave.

Woodland Ave.

Raritan
Rd.

620

South Ave.

E.7th St

Rahway Rd.

605

Johnston Dr.

Mountain Ave.

531

22

Watchung Ave.

601

PLAINFIELD

531

509

N

0   1   2 Miles

0.0 RIGHT onto Springfield Avenue.

After crossing the small bridge near the park entrance, walk your bike across the road. Continue straight ahead along the gravel path; a stream is to your immediate left and a large nursery is on the right.

0.1 Continue STRAIGHT ahead on the paved bicycle path.

This paved trail is also used by joggers and hikers. At 0.2 mile you'll come to a pretty pond on your left and will see stands of cattails on the right.

1.0 CROSS Kenilworth Boulevard and turn LEFT, taking the bicycle path.

The path circles through Nomahegan Park. Cycling along, you'll pass several places with bike route signs pointing in one direction; bear right whenever a choice is presented. You'll come to the first right turn at about 1.1 miles; the path will take you along a quiet, tree-lined street into Cranford.

Architecture buffs might want to detour here to look over some of the Gothic Revival houses such as the charming house found at 110 Holly Street. Sometimes called the pointed style, Gothic Revival's lines carry the eye upward to a steep gabled roof edged with carpenter's lace bargeboards and clustered chimneys. You may want to stretch at one of the fitness stations along this route.

1.8 RIGHT across a wooden bridge over the Rahway River; then take the next TWO RIGHT TURNS.

The trail follows a small scenic pond. During the summer, water lilies, pickerelweed, and the weeping willows growing pondside are a welcome sight, along with the sounds of chirping birds overhead. This is a good rest spot for a snack, and rest rooms are available.

2.3 LEFT off the bike route; CROSS Springfield Avenue into the entrance to Union County College.

Cranford's Union College was the first junior college in the United States to be established with federal funds. Follow the college road as it weaves through the campus—past students and Canada geese on the vast lawns—keeping an eye peeled for its continuation on

The William Miller Sperry Observatory on the grounds of Cranford's Union College is open to the public certain days to observe the heavens.

the other side of Parking Area 2. Here it passes the William Miller Sperry Observatory, open certain days to observe the heavens. For hours, call 908-276-7827.

3.4 RIGHT at the T onto Gallows Hill Road.

Pass a cemetery on the right and the attractive Holy Trinity Greek Orthodox Church on the left. In 1782 convicted murderer James Morgan was hanged on Gallows Hill Road. Considerate of nearby spectators, his last words to the hangman were, "Do your duty and don't keep these folks shivering in the cold."

3.6 LEFT onto St. Marks Avenue.

This is one of Westfield's lovely streets with well-kept houses and large, old trees. Paul Robeson played baseball and basketball at Westfield High for a couple of years around 1910, while Mary Pickford was busy making silent movies here.

4.2 RIGHT onto South Chestnut Street.

4.4 LEFT at the T onto East Broad Street, then an immediate RIGHT onto North Chestnut Street.

5.1 LEFT at the T onto Mountain Avenue.

On the left, at 5.3 miles, is the Miller-Cory House (614 Mountain Avenue), dating to the 1700s. This farmhouse, now a museum staffed by volunteers in period dress, is open only on Sunday afternoons from September to early June. Cooking, crafts, and other day-to-day activities of the early residents are demonstrated; fee; call 201-232-1776 for more information.

Farther down the avenue, just before the junction with East Broad Street, is the historic Presbyterian church.

6.0 RIGHT onto East Broad Street.

Along Broad, you'll pass the castlelike Methodist church on your right, followed by a World War I memorial, before entering a railroad underpass.

BEAR RIGHT immediately afterward.

6.5 LEFT onto West Broad Street.

7.9 LEFT onto Martine Avenue.

This is a busy, wide road.

8.3 RIGHT onto Cooper Street.

There are lots of trees and stately houses along this quiet street in Scotch Plains, named for the Scots who first settled here in the late 1600s.

8.9 LEFT at the traffic light onto Terrill Road.

9.4 RIGHT onto Raritan Road.

USE CAUTION: This road is narrow and curving. You'll pass the entrance to a zoo on the right. On the left is the huge Ash Brook Golf Course, a mecca for golfers and birdwatchers.

10.4 RIGHT onto Rahway Road.

This road, narrow and a bit rough in places, has many large old trees and spacious houses. At 10.9 miles you'll begin to climb a long, steep grade.

11.7 RIGHT onto Woodland Avenue.

12.5 RIGHT onto East Seventh Street.

12.7 LEFT onto Leland Avenue.

Pass a Burger King at the junction with South Avenue.

ALTERNATE ROUTE: To short-circuit this trip and return to the starting point, turn RIGHT onto East Third Street; continue straight on Midway Avenue; turn LEFT at the T onto North Avenue; LEFT onto Dudley Avenue; LEFT onto Mountain Avenue; then take Park Drive (on the right) into Echo Lake Park. To continue the entire trip, however, follow the directions below.

13.9 LEFT at the T onto Mountain Avenue.

Look for the "elf" house, with a large clock on its right side, at the junction with Norwood Avenue.

15.1 RIGHT onto Watchung Avenue.

15.2 LEFT onto a ramp for a bridge crossing Route 22 and then LEFT at the bridge exit, following signs to Watchung.

15.6 RIGHT onto Johnston Drive.

This road is very steep, narrow, curving, and in generally poor condition; it's the most difficult section of road on the trip and a real challenge. After about 1 mile of climbing, pull to the right side for your reward: a rest, a drink, and a view of the towns you have pedaled through. Here, all of eastern New Jersey stretches before you on the plain below. Church steeples and houses seem to poke through gaps in the trees. The houses atop Johnston Drive have nicely forested lots, each is different, and a few are perched on the hillside with commanding views. Continue along Johnston Drive. The road begins to head gently downhill at first, but then it becomes much steeper.

18.8 RIGHT onto Bonnie Burn Road, then a quick LEFT onto New Providence Road.

USE EXTREME CAUTION: Traffic is fast; many accidents have taken place at these intersections. A mining operation comes into view on the left as the road climbs steadily and steeply, and there's a pretty waterfall on the right before the next turn.

19.9 RIGHT onto Valley Road.

The name changes to Sky Top Drive. It's a steep climb for the first mile as the road winds through the Watchung Reservation. The setting is magnificent, and in summer the large trees offer wonderful shade, although it's somewhat dark here even in the middle of a sunny day. During the fall you'll see a rainbow of color along this road as the leaves turn, but no matter when you come, there's a good chance of spotting deer.

22.7 *LEFT at the entrance to the parking lot for the Trailside Museum.*

Inside the museum, you can fill up your canteen, use the rest room, and view the changing exhibits, including a mineral collection, shells, and other artifacts. (Open 1–5; free.)

When you're ready to resume the tour, return to the road and turn LEFT, continuing in the same direction as before; the road name changes to Summit Lane.

23.3 *RIGHT at the circle; take the second road (toward Summit).*

24.1 *STRAIGHT across Summit Road, onto High Point Drive.*

You're now cycling through Springfield Township. During the Battle of Springfield in 1780, when local soldiers ran out of gun wadding, the Reverend James Caldwell cleverly gave them a bunch of hymn books. No, the pages weren't used for singing—but to make gun wadding!

24.4 *Jog LEFT onto Highlands Avenue, then immediately RIGHT to continue on High Point Drive.*

24.6 *RIGHT onto Green Hill Road.*

24.9 *RIGHT onto Tree Top Drive, then an immediate LEFT onto Mountview Road.*

Pedal uphill and then enjoy a steep downhill ride. USE CAUTION, because the road leads abruptly to the Shunpike intersection.

25.9 *RIGHT at the T onto Shunpike Road.*

26.8 *Bear RIGHT onto South Springfield Avenue.*

Stay on this road as it continues weaving on. It passes several stores and gas stations. Be careful crossing Route 22 at 27.3 miles because cars exit quickly.

28.6 *RIGHT onto Mill Lane into Echo Lake Park.*

107

14
Raritan River

Location: Somerset County
Starting point: Raritan Valley Community College, north of Route 22, Branchburg
Terrain: Somewhat hilly
Traffic: Light
Round-trip distance pedaled: 36.1 miles
Highlights: Scenic river, farmland vistas, historic houses and roads, flea market

The Raritan River was recognized by writers and poets way back in the 1600s for both its beauty and its commercial importance. The Native Americans, however, had discovered it long before—naming it Laletan, meaning "forked river"—and used it as their chief route of travel by canoe until the mid-18th century, when Dutch settlers arrived and harnessed sections of the river to power the wheels of gristmills.

Thid trip traverses both the North Branch and South Branch of the Raritan, passing near the area where the two join to form the Raritan River. There is also an opportunity to see two historic homes and a flea market.

The tour begins at the lovely campus of Raritan Valley Community College, formerly Somerset County College, located north of Route 22 in Branchburg. Take Campus Drive from Route 614 and **park** in lot 5. From here you'll be high on a hill facing a picturesque countryside. Set your odometer to 0.0 at the stop sign as you exit from the parking lot.

0.0 RIGHT onto the access road, then LEFT at two Ys onto Campus Drive.

Go downhill, following the main road back to the campus en-

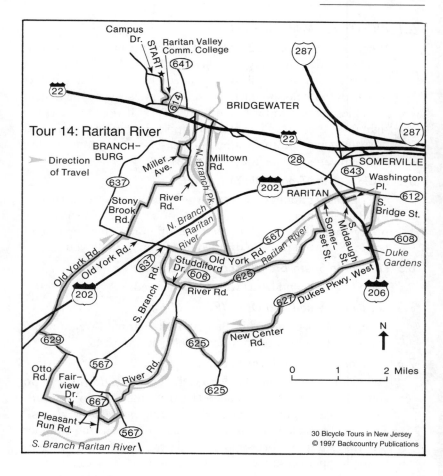

Tour 14: Raritan River

30 Bicycle Tours in New Jersey
© 1997 Backcountry Publications

trance. At 0.6 mile there will be a building on the left and a small duck pond on the right.

0.9 LEFT at the T onto Route 614 east.

Crossing the North Branch of the Raritan River along this level road, you'll enter Bridgewater Township at 1.9 miles. Native Americans traveled this river until the mid-18th century; today the North Branch, which begins in Morris County, is used by modern-day pleasure canoeists.

2.1 RIGHT onto Milltown Road.

When crossing Route 22 USE CAUTION; it's an extremely dangerous divided highway with fast-moving traffic. You'll pass a cornfield on the left; while this stretch of the road has little traffic, it's narrow with no shoulder. The road veers sharply to the right at 3.1 miles at the sign for North Branch Park. If you're here at the right time, firemen will be practicing pole climbing, jumping, and other maneuvers at the nearby Firemen's Training Center. It's fun to watch. Cross Route 202 at 4.0 miles.

5.2 RIGHT at the T onto Old York Road.

After pedaling uphill for a while, you'll cross the North Branch of the Raritan River for the second time at 6.0 miles. This is a very pretty spot where you can look out upon a scenic expanse of farms. It's a good place to open your canteen or dunk your feet.

6.5 LEFT onto South Branch Road (Route 567).

Farm buildings and barns with silos lie ahead.

7.3 LEFT onto Studdiford Drive (Route 606).

Here you'll cross the South Branch of the Raritan River, a pretty stream that's popular with trout anglers and canoeists.

7.6 LEFT at the T onto River Road.

Follow the lovely South Branch north as it heads downstream to converge with the North Branch at a place the Native Americans called Tucca-Ramma-Hacking, "the meeting place of the waters." This nicely shaded area is a cool place to rest during summer months. After a short stretch beside the river, the road goes through open country, affording a feeling of spaciousness. Although this scenic stretch of road has no shoulder, there is barely any traffic. You will encounter some hills before coming next to the river again; where the North Branch and South Branch meet, the river is officially known as the Raritan. Find a tree to sit under and enjoy the view before crossing the one-lane bridge over the Raritan at 11.5 miles.

11.7 RIGHT onto Somerset Street (Route 626).

Many stores offering food and drink line this busy street in the town of Raritan. Stop in at St. Paul's Evangelical Lutheran Church, at the corner of Doughty Street, to see its beautiful stained-glass windows. At the traffic light at 12.3 miles, cross Highway 206.

12.5 RIGHT onto South Middaugh Street and LEFT onto Washington Place.

Take an hour off for a free guided tour through the historic Old Dutch Parsonage (38 Washington Place) and the Wallace House located on this street. Feel free to lock your bicycle in the parking area; the curator generously offers cyclists use of the rest rooms.

The parsonage was built in 1751 for John Frelinghuysen, minister of the Dutch Reformed churches in the Raritan Valley. Here, Frelinghuysen established a theological seminary where young men could be trained for the ministry. When Frelinghuysen died three years later at the age of 27, his wife married Jacob Hardenbergh, one of his young students who later became a Dutch Reformed minister. A staunch supporter of the patriotic cause, occasionally entertaining General George Washington at the parsonage, Hardenbergh also drafted, circulated, and submitted a petition to the Royal government to establish a new "classical and divinity" school in the Colony of New Jersey. The result was the 1766 chartering of Queen's College—now known as Rutgers, the state university. Years later, Hardenbergh became Queen's first president.

At the Wallace House, completed in 1776, you'll learn about John Wallace, a Philadelphia fabric importer and merchant who rented half of his home to General Washington during the winter of 1778–79 for $1000. (Both the Wallace House and the Old Dutch Parsonage are closed on Monday and Tuesday and state and federal holidays. Open hours may vary; call 908-725-1015 before going.) Afterward, retrace the route you came along Washington Place.

12.8 RIGHT onto South Middaugh Street, then RIGHT onto Somerset Street.

The road joins Somerville's main thoroughfare (Route 28). At 13.3 miles stands the attractive old stone United Reformed Church.

13.5 RIGHT onto South Bridge Street.

14.2 LEFT onto Route 206.

The bridge at Neshanic Station leads to the Neshanic flea market, held weekends.

USE CAUTION and stay to the right because traffic is usually heavy here. The entrance to Duke Gardens is on the right.

Tobacco tycoon James Buchanan Duke bought 400 acres of land along the banks of the Raritan in 1893 and by the turn of the century had increased his holdings to 2200 acres. His daughter, Doris, inherited his millions and eventually turned the estate into magnificent enclosed greenhouse gardens open to the public. (Closed summer months; admission fee.)

14.9 RIGHT onto Dukes Parkway West.

Pedaling on this scenic road, which eventually becomes Route 627, is a pleasure. At 17.8 miles it turns sharply to the right, becomes New Center Road, and passes through a rural area with lots of farms and fields.

19.6 RIGHT at the T onto Route 625.

This traffic-free section is bumpy and shoulderless.

21.0 LEFT at the T onto River Road.

Cross the South Branch at 21.9 miles on this level, scenic stretch. At 23.0 miles, cross the South Branch again.

23.5 LEFT at the T onto Route 567.

The South Branch is to your right.

23.7 RIGHT across an iron one-lane bridge.

You've entered quaint Neshanic Station. On weekends, just after crossing the bridge you may pass by while the Neshanic flea market merchants are still selling their fresh fruit, old tools, books, and assorted other goodies. A nearby snack bar provides refreshments and a rest room; you can fill your canteen here.

24.1 RIGHT onto Pleasant Run Road (Route 667).

24.3 LEFT onto Fairview Drive.

You'll encounter a steep hill at the beginning of this stretch. Follow the road as it bends sharply to the right, continuing straight ahead as its name changes to Otto Road. This shoulderless section is very narrow; it offers nice views of fields, cows, and houses along the left.

26.6 LEFT at the T onto Route 629.

27.4 RIGHT onto Old York Road.

As you turn right, a historic marker designates that you're in Centerville on historic Old Post Road, halfway between Philadelphia, Pennsylvania, and Elizabethtown, New Jersey. Back in the 1700s the Swift-Sure Stage Coach Line stopped here overnight.

A steep hill lies ahead. At 27.9 miles, cross Route 202 continuing straight ahead, up and down hills, still on Old York Road.

30.3 RIGHT at the T, continuing on Old York Road.

30.4 LEFT onto Stony Brook Road.

This stretch, through suburban neighborhoods with hardly any traffic and gentle bends, is very enjoyable.

32.7 LEFT at the T onto River Road.

You haven't made a mistake! This is one of the three roads you've passed on this trip with the same name.

32.8 LEFT onto Miller Avenue.

33.4 RIGHT at the T onto Route 637.

At 34.1 miles, cross under Highway 22.

34.4 LEFT at the T onto Route 614.

35.2 RIGHT entering the grounds of Raritan Valley Community College.

The climb is steady as you follow the campus road.

36.1 REACH the starting point.

114

15
Princeton

Location: *Somerset and Mercer Counties*
Starting point: *Colonial Park, Mettler's Road, East Millstone*
Terrain: *Mostly flat; some hills*
Traffic: *Light*
Round-trip distance pedaled: *51.6 miles*
Highlights: *Princeton University campus, Colonial Park, Delaware and Raritan Canal, historic towns, the Millstone River, and Lake Carnegie*

Many of the quaint, quiet towns you'll be visiting on this trip have changed very little since 1777, when Washington and his troops passed through. Get an early start so you can visit the many historic sites and interesting locales along the way as well as linger alongside three serene bodies of water—Lake Carnegie, the Delaware and Raritan Canal, and the Millstone River—that you'll be passing.

Park at Colonial Park near the village of East Millstone, in the parking lot next to the arboretum and adjoining Van der Goot Rose Garden, reachable via Mettler's Road from Amwell Road (Route 514).

Before starting, you may wish to limber up by strolling through the award-winning 1-acre rose garden that features more than 4000 rosebushes, including hybrid tea, grandiflora, floribunda, climbing, miniature, old-fashioned, and botanical roses. (Open sunrise to sunset; free.) A fast walk through the arboretum is also a treat; specimens include dwarf conifers, lilacs, and Japanese flowering cherries.

Reset your odometer at the entrance to the rose garden.

0.0 STRAIGHT, returning to Mettler's Road.

0.1 LEFT onto Mettler's Road, then an immediate RIGHT onto the bike path.

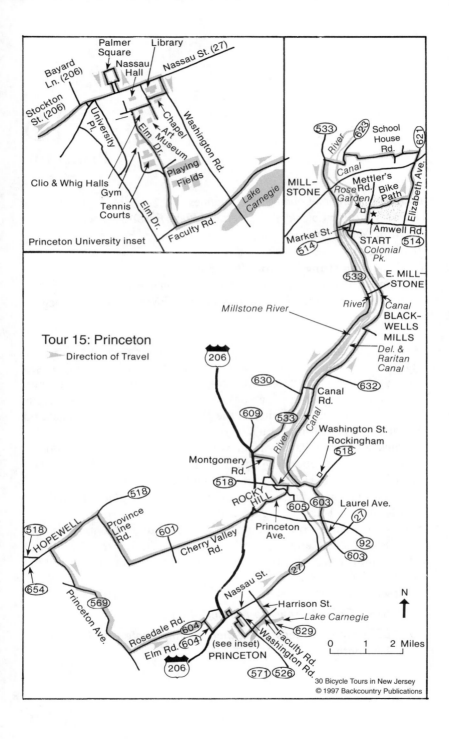

Princeton University inset

Palmer Square
Library
Nassau Hall
Bayard Ln. (206)
Nassau St. (27)
Stockton St. (206)
University Pl.
Chapel
Art Museum
Elm Dr.
Washington Rd.
Playing Fields
Clio & Whig Halls
Gym
Tennis Courts
Elm Dr.
Faculty Rd.
Lake Carnegie

533
623
School House Rd.
621
River
Canal
MILL-STONE
Mettler's Rose Rd.
Bike Path
Elizabeth Ave.
Rose Garden
Market St.
514
Amwell Rd.
START
514
Colonial Pk.
533
E. MILL-STONE
Millstone River
River
Canal
BLACK-WELLS MILLS
Del. & Raritan Canal

Tour 15: Princeton
Direction of Travel

206
630
632
Canal Rd.
609
533
Canal
River
Washington St.
Rockingham
518
Montgomery Rd.
518
ROCKY HILL
605
603
Laurel Ave.
518
Province Line Rd.
27
92
HOPEWELL
601
Cherry Valley Rd.
Princeton Ave.
603
518
654
569
Princeton Ave.
27
Nassau St.
Rosedale Rd.
604
604
Harrison St.
Lake Carnegie
629
Elm Rd.
(see inset)
PRINCETON
Faculty Rd.
Washington Rd.
206
571
526

N

0   1   2 Miles

30 Bicycle Tours in New Jersey
© 1997 Backcountry Publications

This path leads to many activities within the park, including tennis, golf, and a special Par Course Fitness Circuit. The pretty ponds, surrounded by pine trees and weeping willows, are usually teeming with ducks and geese.

1.4 LEFT at the T onto Elizabeth Avenue.

2.8 LEFT onto School House Road.

This narrow road is nearly traffic-free on weekends.

4.9 LEFT at the T onto (unmarked) Route 623.

Stay with this road as it crosses the Delaware and Raritan Canal and then the Millstone River.

5.7 LEFT at the T onto Route 533.

Food and drink are available at 7.8 miles. This pleasant country lane becomes very scenic after its junction with Route 514. The northerly flowing Millstone River almost touches the road. During fall, the foliage resembles an artist's palette.

15.6 LEFT at the T onto Route 206, then an immediate LEFT on Montgomery Road.

Stay on Montgomery Road as it swings into quiet Rocky Hill, settled in 1701.

17.1 LEFT onto Washington Street.

Here you'll pass the First Reformed Church, built in 1857, and places to buy a snack or lunch.

17.3 RIGHT at the First Aid Squad onto (unmarked) Princeton Avenue.

Fields and many large homes line this road. When you come to Route 206 again (at 18.5 miles), drinks and rest rooms are available at a gas station. After crossing this intersection, the road name changes to Cherry Valley Road. During summer months, a canopy of leaves overhead provides relief from the heat.

22.4 RIGHT onto Province Line Road.

Pedaling here is equivalent to being on a roller coaster.

24.1 LEFT onto Route 518.

This road takes you into Hopewell, which has stayed much the same as it was when founded in 1706. The gingerbread houses are an architecture buff's delight.

25.5 LEFT onto Princeton Avenue, Route 569.

The park on the right at about 25.75 miles is perfect for taking a break. Farther down the road you'll find the Educational Testing Service, creator of the dreaded college entrance examinations.

29.9 LEFT onto Rosedale Road (Route 604) into Princeton.

Settled by Quakers on land William Penn purchased in 1693, Princeton's lush, tree-lined streets beckoned dozens of wealthy people, including Grover Cleveland, at the turn of the century.

32.3 RIGHT onto Elm Road, staying with Route 604.

32.8 LEFT onto Route 206 (north).

As you get into the downtown area, look to your left for the Battle Monument, a local landmark. Nearby stands Morven, a circa-1750 Georgian-style mansion that served for many years as the home of New Jersey governors.

33.4 STRAIGHT onto what is now Route 27.

33.5 LEFT onto Palmer Square East.

Thinking it would hurt local businesses, many people opposed Princeton businessman Edgar Palmer's desire to knock down a 12-square-block area in 1935 to erect Palmer Square, a group of fancy shops. Not only did his venture prove highly successful, but also the square has grown in recent years and boasts numerous elegant shops that are perfect for browsing as well as fantastic sculpture by E. Seward Johnson.

When you're finished cycling around the square, turn RIGHT toward the one-way traffic sign, and keep making LEFT turns until you come to Palmer Square West. Follow this street out, back to Nassau Street.

33.8 LEFT onto Nassau Street (Route 27).

You'll find numerous shops where you can browse or purchase food and drink. On your right is Princeton University.

34.0 RIGHT onto Washington Road.

Turn right onto the first walkway in less than 0.1 mile. The John Foster Dulles Library of Diplomatic History on the right stands opposite an unusual sculpture. Carry your bicycle up the ramp in front of you, on the left side of the staircase, for a look at the im-

The Princeton University Art Museum has an impressive 16-foot-high Picasso sculpture, *Head of a Woman*, outside.

pressive *Song of the Vowels* sculpture.

Bike racks, available at this location, can be used if you want to walk over to the Gothic-style University Chapel and nearby buildings. The chapel, dedicated in 1928, can seat more than 2000 people on pews made from army surplus wood originally designated for Civil War gun carriages. The oak paneling, carved in England from Sherwood Forest trees, is from the same wood Robin Hood may have used. On sunny days you'll be able to appreciate the grandeur of the stained-glass windows within the chapel.

To continue by bike, turn left, crossing in front of the chapel. Choose the path that takes you to the left of the Theater in Time.

Farther ahead, slightly to the right, is the University Art Museum and its marvelous outdoor, 16-foot-high Picasso sculpture, *Head of a Woman,* demonstrating the qualities of Cubism for which Picasso is famous. Housing collections of Old Master prints and drawings, Chinese and early Italian paintings, and pre-Columbian art, this museum is definitely worth a stop.

When you've finished your cultural pit stop, take the path leading straight away from the museum entrance and stay on it as it turns left to Nassau Hall.

This stone building, considered one of the largest buildings in the colonies, played an important role in our nation's history. Not only did Nassau Hall survive attack during the Battle of Princeton in 1777, but it also served as the nation's temporary capital when the Continental Congress convened here in 1783. Used for nearly half a century to hold Princeton's classrooms, dormitories, library, chapel, dining room, and kitchen, it now houses the university's offices.

Opposite stand Whig and Clio Halls, designed in marble and erected in 1893 for the American Whig and Cliosophic Society, the nation's oldest college literary and debating clubs. The two societies have since merged, and the halls are now used for student debates and speakers.

Continue ahead, turning LEFT at the corner of Elm Drive, cycling past several buildings, including the gymnasium, tennis courts, and playing fields.

35.0 LEFT onto Faculty Road.

This road takes you past Lake Carnegie, a good place to rest, have a snack, or watch boating activities. The 3.5-mile-long lake, formed by damming Stony Brook and the Millstone River at Kingston, was a gift to the university from industrialist Andrew Carnegie in 1906. Carnegie, upset by the injuries suffered by football players, hoped rowing would become the new sport. The lake's 2000-yard course is considered one of the finest in the East.

35.9 LEFT onto Harrison Street.

36.5 RIGHT onto Nassau Street.

Lake Carnegie shortly comes into view again. As you enter the quaint town of Kingston, you'll see the Millstone River on one side and the Delaware and Raritan Canal on the other. The canal, scooped out by Irish immigrants using picks and shovels, was built to transport Pennsylvania coal. At the canal's height in 1866, mules along the towpath pulled more than 100 barges a day; by 1932, the canal was abandoned because of the railroad. Now a state park, it is used for bicycling, hiking, bird-watching, and canoeing.

38.8 LEFT onto Laurel Avenue, Route 603, at the traffic light.

Prepare for a long uphill climb.

40.4 RIGHT onto Route 518.

40.9 LEFT at the entrance to Rockingham.

General Washington stayed here as a guest of the Berriens while he drafted his "Farewell Orders to the Army." (The mansion is open Wednesday, Friday, and Saturday; free.)

41.1 RIGHT onto Route 518.

After about 0.5 mile you'll begin a refreshing, long downhill stretch.

42.0 RIGHT onto Canal Road.

The Delaware and Raritan Canal is on your left along this entire stretch. The maples turn brilliant colors during autumn in this area. You'll soon pass Griggstown—don't worry about exceeding the weight limit on the one-lane bridge at 47.0 miles unless you've had a huge lunch.

47.3 Jog LEFT, then RIGHT at a T and continue on Canal Road.

Blackwells Mills, at 48.6 miles, and several other towns along the canal were active during the days when the canal was a main route for commerce. You'll come to the end of Canal Road in the tiny community of East Millstone where the road suddenly curves to the right, leaving you on Elm Street.

50.5 LEFT onto Market Street.

50.7 RIGHT at the T onto Amwell Road.

51.1 LEFT onto Mettler's Road.

51.5 LEFT at the entrance to the arboretum parking lot in Colonial Park.

The entrance to the rose garden is just ahead at 51.6 miles.

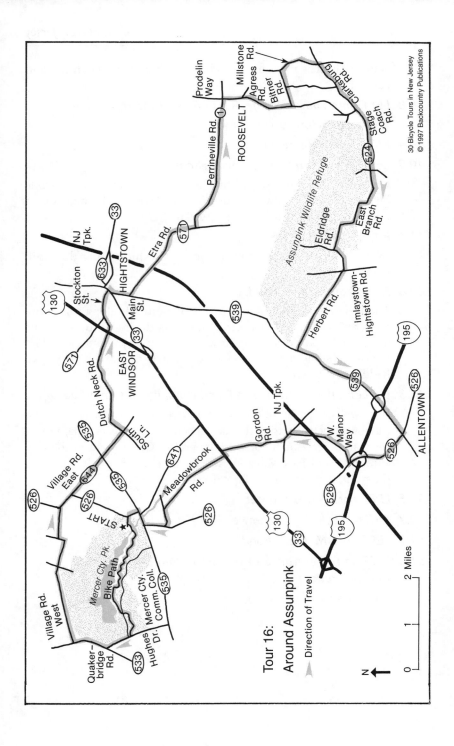

Tour 16:
Around Assunpink

➤ Direction of Travel

30 Bicycle Tours in New Jersey
© 1997 Backcountry Publications

16
Around Assunpink

Location: *Mercer and Monmouth Counties*
Starting point: *Mercer County Park, off Route 526, Edinburg*
Terrain: *Mostly flat*
Traffic: *Light*
Round-trip distance pedaled: *40.0 miles*
Highlights: *Horse and sheep farms, fishing, Victorian architecture, bird-watching*

Hurry to take this trip while the area still retains so much of its rural charm. Many communities have been recently built, and dozens of houses are under construction, but this easy trip traverses sections of Mercer and Monmouth Counties where there's still some undeveloped farmland and wooded areas. Mercer County Park, the county's showplace, offers an excellent, scenic bicycle trail to limber up on at the beginning of the trip.

Within the Assunpink Fish and Wildlife Management Area are five man-made lakes stocked with catfish, largemouth bass, sunfish, and pickerel. Although hunting and fishing are emphasized, Assunpink is considered one of the best birding areas in central New Jersey. If you bring binoculars along, you may spot a turkey vulture, hawk, warbler, or sparrow. During the fall, hunters can usually be seen stalking the abundant deer, rabbits, squirrels, and grouse that roam freely through the refuge.

Park at the East Picnic Area in Mercer County Park off Route 526, just west of its junction with Route 535 in the hamlet of Edinburg.

0.0 STRAIGHT on the paved bike trail through Mercer County Park.

The trail begins at the edge of the parking area and meanders through this 2500-acre park, which includes picnic areas, playgrounds, tennis courts, playing fields, and a lovely lake used for canoeing, sailing, and rowing. You'll pass huge oak trees and a blanket of wildflowers during spring and summer months, and you'll likely spot squirrels and chipmunks as they dart out along the path. Head straight ahead when in doubt about which way to go.

3.3 RIGHT at the end of the bicycle path onto Hughes Drive.

4.0 RIGHT at the T onto Quakerbridge Road.

4.7 RIGHT onto Village Road West (which becomes Village Road East).

This smooth road goes past open fields and houses. Stay with it as it turns sharply. Cross Route 535 at 9.1 miles.

9.8 LEFT onto South Lane.

Continue on this road as it turns into Dutch Neck Road, which then passes through an East Windsor housing development.

12.7 RIGHT onto Stockton Street (Route 571) in Hightstown.

Many wealthy people moved to Hightstown during the mid-1850s because of its location midway between Perth Amboy and Burlington. Stockton Street has prime examples of the fine Victorian houses built here during that period.

13.2 RIGHT at the T onto Main Street. Stay LEFT, taking Route 571.

Peddie School and several mansions are on the left.

13.7 LEFT, still following Route 571 (Etra Road).

The road is narrow here but in good shape. After passing Etra Lake on the left, stay with Route 571 as it makes some sharp turns.

17.0 LEFT onto Perrineville Road (Monmouth County Route 1).

It's slow going while pedaling uphill, but the farms provide nice scenery to take your mind off aching muscles. Continue on this road as it makes a sharp right just before Prodelin Way comes in on the left.

19.2 Bear RIGHT onto Agress Road.

You're now skirting the municipality of Roosevelt. In the 1930s a factory and dozens of flat-roofed cinder-block houses were built as a social experiment in cooperative living for needle-trade workers. The village never succeeded as a self-sufficient commu-

You'll see grazing horses throughout your trip around Assunpink.

nity, but today Roosevelt looks much the same as it did originally and is home to many writers and artists.

20.3 LEFT onto Bitner Road.

21.2 RIGHT at the T onto Millstone Road.

Horse farms abound; if you pull over to a fenced pasture for a closer view, one of the horses will usually come over.

22.1 RIGHT onto Clarksburg Road.

The road climbs steeply at first; it's narrow with a sand shoulder.

23.3 Bear RIGHT onto Stage Coach Road.

You're now in the midst of sheep farms.

25.3 RIGHT onto East Branch Road.

The road takes you through a stretch of pretty country as it crosses a corner of the Assunpink Wildlife Refuge, a 5400-acre reservation managed by the New Jersey Department of Environmental Protection's Division of Fish, Game, and Wildlife. At the center of the refuge are man-made lakes that support a warm-water fish population, including largemouth bass and chain pickerel. Unfortunately, you'll have to walk to the lake because the park road is too rocky to cycle over.

East Branch Road twists sharply in places. At 26.8 miles it turns sharply to the left as Eldridge Road comes in from the right.

27.4 Go STRAIGHT through the intersection with (unmarked) Imlaystown-Hightstown Road.

This will take you onto Herbert Road.

29.5 LEFT at the T onto Route 539 (south).

There is a deli at 31.8 miles. Continue ahead to the center of Allentown.

32.5 RIGHT onto Route 526 (west).

Cross Route 195 and look for the first genuine road (not an entrance or exit for the freeway) on the right. This is West Manor Way. If you come to the New Jersey Turnpike, you've gone too far.

33.8 RIGHT onto (unmarked) West Manor Way.

35.3 LEFT at the T onto Gordon Road.

This smooth, deserted road is very pleasant to pedal on.

36.9 LEFT at the T onto Route 130 (a divided road with heavy traffic); then an immediate RIGHT onto Meadowbrook Road.

39.0 RIGHT at the T onto Route 526.

39.4 RIGHT at the T, then LEFT in about 0.2 mile, still following Route 526.

39.8 LEFT at the entrance to the East Picnic Area of Mercer County Park.

The parking area is just ahead at 40.0 miles.

17
Rutgers

Location: Middlesex Country
Starting point: Johnson Park, Olde Towne section off River Road,
   Piscataway
Terrain: Mostly flat
Traffic: Moderate during week; light on weekends
Round-trip distance pedaled: 9.0 miles
Highlights: Rutgers, the state university, at the Busch and Livingston
   campuses; stadium; Johnson Park, zoo, and East Jersey Olde Towne

You don't have to be enrolled at Rutgers, the state university, to enjoy this tour. You will be pedaling not only through the Busch and Livingston campuses, but also through Johnson Park. Plan this trip on a weekend to avoid heavy traffic. Hours at East Jersey Olde Towne are variable, depending on the budget, but feel free to roam around even when the buildings are closed; call 732-247-4006 for specific dates and times that events are held here.

Park in the Olde Towne parking lot off River Road in Piscataway along Johnson Drive opposite Hoes Lane. If you like, spend a while limbering up while exploring the village. Consisting of 20 buildings that originally stood in various parts of central New Jersey, the village shows what life was like for English and Dutch farmers during the Revolutionary War period. Among the houses are the circa-1743 FitzRandolph house, which is the type a farmer new to the area would have built; the circa-1745 Dunn Farmhouse, a house typical of those owned by successful farmers; and the 1780 Runyon House, a mansion containing 17 rooms.

Dr. Joseph Kier got the idea for assembling the restored 19th-century village after learning that the Indian Queen Tavern, a historic New Brunswick meeting place built in 1686, was going to be torn down. He

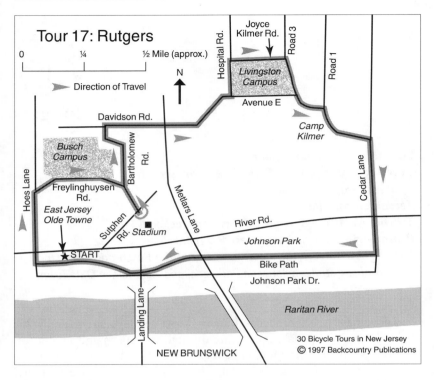

Tour 17: Rutgers

0   ¼   ½ Mile (approx.)

N

Direction of Travel

Joyce Kilmer Rd.

Road 3

Road 1

Hospital Rd.

Livingston Campus

Avenue E

Camp Kilmer

Cedar Lane

Davidson Rd.

Bartholomew Rd.

Busch Campus

Hoes Lane

Freylinghuysen Rd.

East Jersey Olde Towne

Sutphen Rd.

Stadium

Meilars Lane

River Rd.

Johnson Park

START

Bike Path

Johnson Park Dr.

Landing Lane

Raritan River

30 Bicycle Tours in New Jersey
© 1997 Backcountry Publications

NEW BRUNSWICK

then purchased it for the grand sum of one dollar! Later, Middlesex County wisely set aside several acres of land in Johnson Park to house the village, while money from private sources was used to purchase additional buildings.

When you're ready to start your tour, walk your bike to the fitness track map located to your right as you face Olde Towne's buildings. Set your odometer and begin on the bicycle path in front of you and adjacent to the parking lot toward the left. The buildings will be on the right as you pedal.

0.0 LEFT (west) onto the bike trail, then bear RIGHT.

Off-duty horses used by the park police can usually be seen nibbling the grass inside fenced areas on both sides of the road. The bike trail ends shortly. Cross River Road onto Hoes Lane from the park path.

0.6 RIGHT turn at the first road (Freylinghuysen) just after the golf course entrance.

This is the Busch campus of Rutgers. To the right is the very popular and always busy Rutgers Golf Course. Thankfully, the golfers are usually experienced enough to keep the balls on the green—but if they miss, you'll be wearing your helmet for protection! The impressive building on the left adorned with a clock tower is the Waksman Institute of Microbiology, named in honor of the scientist who pioneered the discovery of several antibiotics. Other buildings include the Center for Advanced Biotechnology and Medicine; the William Levine College of Pharmacy; and the Hill Center for Mathematical Sciences.

1.8 RIGHT onto Sutphen Road.

The impressive football stadium on the left brings in lots of money to the university. You might want to stop for a while if the lacrosse team is practicing in the field on the right; if you're wondering what that huge bubble dome is, it's a modern sports center.

2.0 U-TURN into the parking lot on the left, and turn around the way you came.

2.1 LEFT at the intersection.

Duck fast if you spot a golf ball heading your way; the field to the left is a favorite practice spot for duffers.

2.5 RIGHT at Bartholomew Road.

Another athletic building is on the left. Look for an interesting blue metal sculpture on the right. On the opposite side is the Busch dining hall and a student center. Straight ahead, three tall pipes that are part of a heating system reach toward the sky. Watch for speed bumps in the road, and follow the road where it bends sharply.

3.1 RIGHT onto Davidson Road.

Continue straight, passing through the intersection at Metlars Lane at 3.5 miles. For a short distance, there are patches of dense woods on both sides that can't be developed, because they're part of the Rutgers Ecological Preserve. Lots of birds congregate around the junipers, a species usually found growing in old pastures and poor ground. Birds love to nibble at the blueberry-like fruit that junipers are famous for.

3.9 LEFT onto Hospital Road.

Here you'll find a beautifully designed athletic center and running track.

4.2 RIGHT at Joyce Kilmer Avenue.

As you enter the Livingston College campus, you'll probably spot lots of people skateboard sailing in a large parking lot. Often there are more boarders than cars! Stop for a while to admire the colorful sails or watch the spills. Ouch!

4.7 RIGHT onto Road 3.

Livingston Recreation Area, basketball, and tennis courts are on the left immediately after this turn. Just up ahead are shady picnic sites, perfect for a rest stop or snack.

5.3 RIGHT onto Road 1.

You're now entering Camp Kilmer, an area named in honor of the poet Joyce Kilmer, who was born across the river in New Brunswick in 1886 and killed in action during World War I. The row of buildings resembling corrugated tin are now used as warehouses, but originally they were barracks for enlisted men in the US Army during World War II. It was here that they waited before being sent abroad to see action. Historian David Cowen remembers having been invited to present a lecture to the soldiers on "Opportunities in Education," and how, "five minutes into my talk, the men were so tired from marching over to the building I was in that they fell asleep!"

5.7 RIGHT onto Cedar Lane.

The garden apartments on the left bring back fond memories, since they served as my first residence for 10 years after I moved to New Jersey. Unfortunately, the woods opposite the development have since been replaced with more apartments. However, not all the beauty has disappeared; as you roll down the hill, the Raritan River comes into view straight ahead.

6.2 CROSS River Road and take the bike path on the right side of the road going through Johnson Park.

Benjamin Franklin and John Adams often stopped in at the Indian Queen Tavern, circa 1686. The tavern, purchased by Dr. Kier for one dollar, was the beginning of the East Jersey Olde Town re-created village.

The tall buildings across the river are student dorms. Watch out for crossing geese. They're a hazard throughout the park.

A small zoo is on the right at 7.0 miles. Despite the ugly fence around this zoo, families like to come to admire the animals. This is a nice area to take a break; no doubt you'll have lots of ducks and geese keeping you company and begging for a handout the second they spot your lunch. When you're ready to roll, continue ahead. A row of stately sycamore trees soon appears. Also known as the buttonwood or plane tree, this specimen is blessed with a beautiful mottled brown bark. One of the largest of our native broad-leafed trees, it often reaches a height of 150 feet and drops hundreds of round seed balls onto the ground.

9.0 ARRIVE back at the East Jersey Olde Towne parking lot.

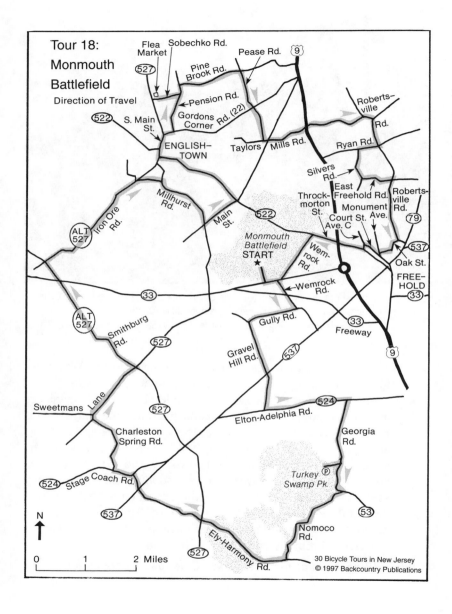

Tour 18:
Monmouth
Battlefield

Direction of Travel

Flea Market
Sobechko Rd.
Pease Rd.
527
Pine Brook Rd.
9
Pension Rd.
Robertsville
522
S. Main St.
Gordons Corner Rd. (22)
ENGLISHTOWN
Taylors Mills Rd.
Ryan Rd.
Rd.
Silvers Rd.
East Freehold Rd.
Robertsville Rd.
Throckmorton St.
Monument Ave.
79
Millhurst Rd.
Iron Ore Rd.
ALT 527
Main St.
522
Court St. Ave. C
537
Monmouth Battlefield START
Wemrock Rd.
Oak St.
FREEHOLD
33
ALT 527
33
Wemrock Rd.
33
Smithburg Rd.
Gully Rd.
Freeway
9
527
Gravel Hill Rd.
531
Sweetmans Lane
527
Elton-Adelphia Rd.
524
Charleston Spring Rd.
Georgia Rd.
524
Stage Coach Rd.
Turkey Swamp Pk.
537
53
N

0   1   2 Miles

Nomoco Rd.
527
Ely-Harmony Rd.

30 Bicycle Tours in New Jersey
© 1997 Backcountry Publications

18
Monmouth Battlefield

Location: *Monmouth County*
Starting point: *Monmouth Battlefield State Park, Route 33,*
   Manalapan Township
Terrain: *Slightly hilly*
Traffic: *Light to moderate*
Round-trip distance pedaled: *41.2 miles*
Highlights: *Monmouth Battlefield State Park, Turkey Swamp State*
   Park, nature trails, paddle boating, fishing, canoeing, flea market, his-
   toric sites

Ready . . . aim . . . *duck*—especially if you take this trip the last weekend in June. That's when troops gather at Monmouth Battlefield State Park to reenact what is considered to be the longest sustained combat of the Revolutionary War. (Call 732-462-9616 for the exact date and time.) Although neither the British nor the Continental Army could clearly claim victory at the end of the battle, both sides deserved a standing ovation for their courage during eye-to-eye combat.

Events leading to this battle began during the spring of 1778, when the British started evacuating Philadelphia after learning that France had sent troops to help the Continental Army. However, the British didn't plan well; not only did they burden themselves by carrying enormous amounts of supplies on a 12-mile-long wagon train, using valuable manpower to safeguard these possessions, but they also suffered under the weight of their heavy packs and uniforms.

Washington (who luckily wasn't sleeping anywhere at the time) quickly assessed the situation. Realizing that his soldiers were well trained, with new uniforms and equipment, he ordered them to put up roadblocks, destroy bridges, and do anything to further weaken the enemy.

You'll be pedaling past ground where Alexander Hamilton, Aaron Burr, Molly Pitcher, and other Revolutionary War heroes fought. Molly was born in New Jersey of German descent in 1754; her real name was Molly Ludwig Hays. When her husband, John Hays, was assigned duty in New Jersey, she stayed with him throughout the battle, helping him and his company by carrying water during the extreme June heat. Soldiers referred to her as "Molly with the pitcher," and the name stuck. When her husband suffered from heat exhaustion and could no longer fire his cannon, she replaced him, later receiving a commendation from Washington and an army pension—long before the women's liberation movement.

Park your car near the visitors center in the large lot at Monmouth Battlefield State Park, off Route 33. Spend some time inside the center, where several automatic color slide presentations and an electronic scale model map of the area depict troop movements during the battle. The center, which overlooks the fields where a great part of the conflict was waged, is open daily 9–4 except on major holidays. Hours are subject to change; although admission is free year-round, donations are requested for special events, including the Battle of Monmouth reenactment.

Limber up before your ride by strolling down Combs Hill and try to imagine what took place here. A bridge crosses the marsh, leading onto the battlefield. If you care to walk farther, try the short nature trail, which is excellent during springtime when skunk cabbage, purple violets, maples, and the songs from resident warblers and frogs create just the right mood before cycling.

Reset your odometer to 0.0 at the stop sign at the exit from the main parking lot.

0.0 STRAIGHT *ahead on the park road toward the entrance on Route 33.*

0.5 LEFT *onto Route 33.*

This road is wide but extremely busy.

0.7 RIGHT *at the first traffic light onto Wemrock Road.*

Wemrock Road is a fairly wide road with moderate traffic. USE EXTREME CAUTION as you cross the Route 33 freeway; an entrance ramp to the highway crosses the right lane, and motorists sometimes enter the ramp at high speed.

1.4 RIGHT onto Gully Road.

This lightly traveled narrow side road has great views of wooded areas and apple orchards.

2.4 Sharp LEFT onto Gravel Hill Road.

Some uphill pedaling is required on the first stretch of this lane. After about 0.5 mile, the road levels out, taking you through open farmland.

4.3 LEFT at the T onto Elton-Adelphia Road.

This is a wide road with moderate traffic changing from farmland to a suburban area.

6.0 RIGHT onto Georgia Road at the sign for Turkey Swamp Park.

7.7 RIGHT at the entrance to Turkey Swamp Park.

8.0 LEFT into the main parking lot, near the park office.

Lock your bike here; rest rooms are available at the side of the building. The park, located on the northern fringe of the Pine Barrens, takes its name from the town of Turkey, now known as Adelphia. The area is unique, according to the Monmouth County Park System brochure, "for although the soil is very sandy, the water table lies just beneath the surface, giving rise to swampy conditions whenever the surface topography dips to the water line; [hence] the 'swamp' in the name Turkey Swamp."

If you wish, you can take a 2-mile bike ride through the park on a gravel maintenance road to get a feel for the area. The land within the park is nearly flat; the geologic formations are composed of sands and clays, providing a habitat for scrub oaks and young white oaks and a thick understory of pepperbush, huckleberry, and blueberry. Tall pitch pines are currently springing up on the fringes of the forest, while sweet gum and aspen also exist in thick stands here.

Should you care to walk through another day, try one of the pleasant, easy trails. My husband and I tried the red trail, about 1.25 miles in length, leading out to the woodsy Wilderness Camping area. There is also a green-blazed, 1-mile trail bordering the red trail, also leading to the lakefront area, and a 0.5-mile blue trail going to the boathouse. You can picnic, fish, canoe, or rent paddleboats. If this bike trip isn't giving you enough exercise, try working out on the new physical fitness trail, which provides a program of cardiovascular conditioning, flexibility routines, and exercises for muscle tone.

After finishing at the park, return to the main parking lot to pick up the mileage and head toward the entrance.

8.3 RIGHT after leaving the park, staying on Nomoco Road.

This pleasant road winds through pine groves, new houses, and Turkey Swamp Park on the right.

10.4 RIGHT at the T onto Ely-Harmony Road.

This long grade will have you puffing, but gentle hills follow. Traffic is light here; there are broad curves and the road levels, passing through more pines, a few farmhouses, residential houses, open fields, and a fruit stand as you cross Route 537.

14.1 LEFT at the T onto (unmarked) Stage Coach Road.

14.4 RIGHT onto Charleston Spring Road.

Start by climbing a small hill. The scenery is pleasant, a mixture of thoroughbred farms, horses, and barns. The route follow a winding, slightly hilly road.

15.9 RIGHT at the T onto (unmarked) Sweetmans Lane.

Follow this uphill for about 0.5 mile on a smooth road past pastureland, although farms are giving way to developments in this area.

17.2 LEFT onto Route 527A (Smithburg Road).

This smooth, level road goes past a tree nursery, horse farms, and houses as you pedal up small hills. Cross Route 33.

20.1 RIGHT, following the sign for Route 527A toward Englishtown.

Though it lacks a sign, this road is identified as Iron Ore Road on the Monmouth County map. It starts uphill, going up and down until it levels out after a long, gentle descent. Open fields may be seen on the left. Stay right on Iron Ore Road at the junction at about 22.5 miles.

23.1 RIGHT at the T onto an unmarked road, then take the next LEFT (after 0.1 mile) onto Millhurst Road.

Woods and some houses are on this pleasant road.

24.4 LEFT onto Main Street, County Route 3.

25.2 LEFT onto Route 522 at the sign for Englishtown.

This road is a bit busy, but it has a narrow, sandy shoulder. Refreshments can be purchased just before the junction with South Main Street in the center of Englishtown.

27.0 RIGHT onto South Main Street.

27.4 RIGHT onto Gordons Corner Road (Route 22).

27.6 LEFT onto Pension Road.

28.4 LEFT onto Sobechko Road.

This road takes you into the famous Englishtown Flea Market. Flea markets were named for the fleas that once occupied every square inch of the areas where merchants sold their wares in open markets. Today the fleas may be gone, but be forewarned: The Englishtown Flea Market—reputed to be the largest in the state— can be a muddy mess after rain or snow. It's best to lock your bike in a dry area and walk around to see the huge amount of goodies for sale. It's always fun, and it's open year-round on Saturday dawn–5 and Sunday 9–5.

When you've finished exploring and shopping, return to the corner of Sobechko and Pension Roads.

28.4 LEFT (north) onto Pension Road from Sobechko Road.

28.6 First RIGHT onto Pine Brook Road.

After climbing a small hill, you'll pass woods that may eventually becomes sites for new houses.

29.9 RIGHT onto Pease Road at the stop sign.

Relatively free of traffic, this is a nicely shaded country road.

31.4 LEFT at the T onto Taylors Mills Road.

After passing through housing developments, cross Route 9 at the stoplight. USE CAUTION: This intersection is usually busy. Here you'll begin pedaling along a wide road through an established suburban area. The road name eventually changes to Lafayette Road.

33.5 RIGHT at the T onto (unmarked) Robertsville Road.

34.2 RIGHT onto (unmarked) Ryan Road.

34.6 LEFT onto Silvers Road.

Traveling these medium-sized hills provides a good workout.

35.3 LEFT onto East Freehold Road.

On this section you will have smooth pedaling in a lovely neighborhood.

35.9 RIGHT onto Robertsville Road.

After passing horse farms, climb up a long, fairly steep hill heading toward the center of the Borough of Freehold.

37.1 RIGHT onto Oak Street.

Follow Oak Street as it curves along.

37.6 LEFT at the T on (unmarked) Monument Avenue.

The Monmouth County Court House is to your right. At the corner of Monument Avenue and Court Street stands the impressive Battle of Monmouth statue, designated a New Jersey state Historic Site. The panels depict scenes from the Revolution, scenes honoring Molly Pitcher, the Wayne Charge, Washington rallying the troops, and the Council of War at Hopewell. It includes such personages as Lafayette, Washington, and Lord Stirling and has an impressive figure at the top. A time capsule is buried near the monument.

Freehold was originally established in 1715 by Scottish settlers who named the area Monmouth and their new village Monmouth Court House. The village quickly gained a reputation as an important agricultural center because the flat land was so fertile. The town was renamed Freehold in 1801.

37.7 RIGHT at the T onto Court Street.

The impressive Georgian-style stone house on your left is the Monmouth County Historical Association. Stop if you wish to see an excellent collection of American antiques, furniture, textiles, ceramics, firearms, and paintings, as well as the research library chock-full of books relating to local history and genealogy. (Open Tuesday through Saturday 10–4 and Sunday 1–4; fee.)

38.0 LEFT onto Avenue C.

38.2 RIGHT onto Throckmorton Street (Route 522).

Plan your ride to coincide with the Battle of Monmouth reenactment the last weekend in June for a big blast!

Before going under the Route 9 underpass, this road traverses an industrial area.

39.4 LEFT onto Wemrock Road.

During apple blossom time these orchards are beautiful; in season you may be able to purchase apples and cider.

40.5 RIGHT onto Route 33.

40.7 RIGHT at the entrance to Monmouth Battlefield State Park.

Continue straight ahead to reach your starting point at 41.2 miles.

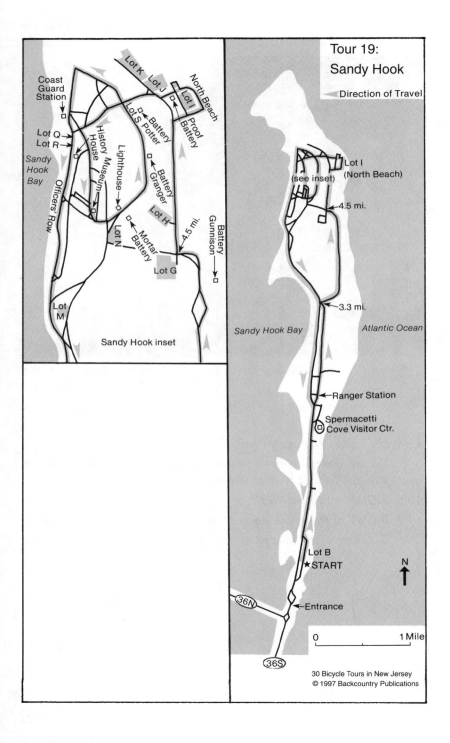

Tour 19:
Sandy Hook

◀ Direction of Travel

Coast Guard Station

Lot K Lot J

North Beach

Lot I

Proof Battery

Lot Q →
Lot R →

Lot S Potter Battery

History Museum House

Lighthouse

Battery Granger

Lot H

Sandy Hook Bay

Officers' Row

Lot N

Mortar Battery

4.5 mi.

Battery Gunnison

Lot G

Lot M

Sandy Hook inset

Lot I
(North Beach)
(see inset)

4.5 mi.

3.3 mi.

Sandy Hook Bay

Atlantic Ocean

Ranger Station

Spermacetti
Cove Visitor Ctr.

Lot B
★ START

N

36N

Entrance

0   1 Mile

36S

30 Bicycle Tours in New Jersey
© 1997 Backcountry Publications

19
Sandy Hook

Location: Monmouth County
Starting point: Sandy Hook, Gateway National Recreation Area, Route 36, Sandy Hook
Terrain: Flat
Traffic: Light
Round-trip distance pedaled: 11.6 miles
Highlights: Lighthouse, fort, holly forest, swimming

Sandy Hook offers easy cycling along beautiful dunes, a quiet bay, and pounding ocean surf. Another bonus in cycling "the Hook" is the opportunity to relive history. Here you can explore an old fort, enter the site of one of the first US Life Saving Service stations on the eastern seaboard, and tour one of the oldest original working lighthouses in the country. Topping this off with a walk in the holly forest or going for a swim guarantees a memorable day.

Although it appears to be a peaceful place now, Sandy Hook has had an eventful history. Between 1839 and 1848, roughly 158 vessels were lost off the Jersey shore. The cry for help—"Ship Ashore!"—was usually futile since there was no plan in effect to save those aboard a foundering ship until Congress finally appropriated money to build small lifeboat stations along the Jersey coast.

Farther along your ride, you'll see why Sandy Hook, strategically located at the entrance to New York Harbor, was an ideal place to build Fort Hancock, with its massive mortar batteries. While the fort looks much the same as it did when soldiers manned it to protect the harbor, the shape of the sandy spit of land it was built on has changed.

Although the Lenni-Lenape found the same fishing grounds and tasty beach plums that we see today, the contours of the Hook keep changing because the ocean carries sand north. The lighthouse originally stood only 500 feet from the water's edge, but it's now about 1.5 miles away because of the strong offshore currents.

The busy season is from Memorial Day to Labor Day, and that's when a fee is charged for parking. Plan on arriving off-season or late in the day when the crowds are gone, and stay to watch the sunset. For information on park programs, call 732-872-0115.

Park in lot B, the first lot after entering the park.

0.0 RIGHT (north) onto the park road.

To your left, perched 254 feet above sea level overlooking Sandy Hook Bay, are the impressive Twin Lights of Navesink. Now a historical and maritime museum, this was once an important lighthouse and radar experimental station. It makes an interesting side trip; call 732-872-1814 for hours.

On the right, sand dunes and huge boulders keep the ocean from encroaching too far onto the land. During summer months, rest rooms and refreshments are found at most parking lot areas.

1.7 RIGHT to Spermaceti Cove Visitor Center.

This is a "must" stop. Pick up a map and information on programs, and before leaving, check out the excellent exhibits in this circa-1894 building detailing the natural history of Sandy Hook and the US Life Saving Service.

During summer months, exciting rescue drills are reenacted here according to government regulations of 1899, complete with period dress and a small bronze cannon once used to fire a line to the ship. The "rescued" people are brought back to land in a breeches buoy: a life preserver with pants attached in which a person sits while being pulled back to safety. It's a thrill to watch, especially the firing of the cannon.

You'll enjoy taking the Old Dune Trail just outside the visitors center. This 1-mile loop trail is reputed to have the largest stand of American hollies on the eastern seaboard. Prickly pear cactus is one of the dominant plants along the walk, and during summer months it shows off spectacular bright yellow flowers. Birds monopolize the hollies during winter, when they can be seen diving down into the bushes to get the luscious red berries. There are lots of beach plums but even more poison ivy, so watch out.

Return to the main road, turn RIGHT, and pass through the gate into Fort Hancock.

Surrounded by Sandy Hook Bay, New York Harbor, and the Atlantic Ocean, Fort Hancock was named for Civil War Major General Winfield Scott Hancock. Enlisted men were garrisoned here in the 1890s, standing watch over gun batteries.

Today the fort looks very much the same as it did in days long gone with every building, street, sidewalk, and bit of lawn planned in advance by the army.

3.3 RIGHT at the sign for North Beach.

Park at Battery Gunnison, about 1.1 miles down the road on the right. Explore the gun emplacements built in 1904 to protect the coast against possible attack and the battery's two 6-inch-caliber guns, which were built on disappearing carriages; in 1943 they were converted to barbette pedestals. Their steel shields protected the gun crews from machine-gun or light-cannon fire, while mines, anchored around the entrance to New York Harbor, could be fired electrically from shore.

4.5 RIGHT at the sign for North Beach.

5.0 RIGHT to Parking Lot I.

Formed since 1900 by the longshore current, North Beach is a good place to swim, spot shorebirds, look for interesting shells, and enjoy the sounds of the ocean.

Follow direction signs out of the lot and continue STRAIGHT ahead.

On the left is Proof Battery, once an integral part of the US Army's Sandy Hook Proving Ground. Here were mounted and tested machine guns, field artillery, heavy artillery, and large-caliber mortars. Even the small bronze Lyle gun, used in shipwreck rescues, was tested at this proving ground, which was in operation from 1874 to 1919.

5.3 RIGHT at the stop sign, then an immediate LEFT.

5.6 LEFT at the stop sign (this is the road just before the street running along the bay).

Pedal past the quarters on the left (on your left as you head south). Sandy Hook Museum is on the left about 0.2 mile down. Through

143

At Sandy Hook, cycle past one of the oldest continuously operating lighthouses in the country.

pictures and authentic historical artifacts, this 1899 guardhouse and post jail now serves as a museum, open weekends 1–5 year-round.

5.9 LEFT at the yield sign.

At the next yield sign, the lighthouse looms on your left and a mortar battery is on your right. This mortar battery, completed in 1894, was the first of its kind used for coastal defense. Once inside, you can follow the railroad tracks into one of the four identical pits connected by a tunnel. The circles on the floor indicate former platforms that once supported large breech-loading mortars.

Unfortunately, the lighthouse is not always open to the public; let's hope it will be when you arrive, because the inside is fascinating. Completed in 1764 to protect ships sailing into New York Harbor, the lighthouse stands an impressive 103 feet tall. To reach the lantern involves a climb of 95 steps plus a 12-foot ladder. While the exterior walls are built of rubble stone, the interior is lined with brick. The walls are over 10 feet thick at the base.

Automated in 1962, the light currently used is a 45,000-candlepower, white electric-fired light that is visible for about 19 miles. In 1964 the lighthouse was declared a National Historic Landmark.

When you are ready to continue the tour, return to the road you were on and turn LEFT after the yield sign in front of the mortar battery.

You'll soon come to Battery Granger and Battery Potter, both on the right side. Although off-limits, they're still impressive to look at, having once served as part of New York Harbor's defense system.

Battery Potter, disarmed in 1906, was the only fortification of its kind in the United States. It contained steam-powered hydraulic equipment to raise and lower guns. Neither weapons nor crew were visible from the ocean. The Battery Granger's two 10-inch-caliber guns could strike a ship 8 miles out at sea.

6.5 RIGHT at the stop sign, then an immediate LEFT.

The entrance to the Coast Guard station is 0.2 mile ahead; visitors, unfortunately, are not allowed. Stay left, cycling south along the bay. At 6.9 miles you'll see the Rodman Gun. This impressive cannon is reputed to be the largest smooth-bore, muzzle-loading weapon ever cast.

Continue straight along "Officer's Row" overlooking Sandy Hook Bay for a look at houses that differ from the usual army quarters. Normally facing the parade ground, here they were built to face the bay.

History House on the left at 7.0 miles is worth a stop. Filled with veterans' memorabilia and photo exhibits, it was built in 1898 and has furnishings and housewares common to an officer's home from 1900 to 1945. (Open weekends 1–5 year-round.)

7.6 RIGHT at the yield sign; follow the main park road south.

You'll pass many of the same plants the Native Americans probably used as food and medicine: yarrow, for burns and earaches; cattails, for food and padding in pillows; prickly pear cactus, to remove warts; phragmites, enjoyed for its special gum extract; joe-pye weed, used as a stimulant; and black cherry, which they dried and preserved.

Stop at the small picnic area on the right at 8.1 miles for a short walk along a spit of land protruding into the bay, a favorite hangout for the birds. Your bike can be locked to the boardwalk fence.

There's a good chance that you'll see lots of birds; the Hook is located along the Atlantic Flyway, and more than 300 avian species have been spotted here.

Continue STRAIGHT ahead back to the starting point.

20
Allaire

Location: *Monmouth County*
Starting point: *Allaire State Park, Allaire Road (Route 524), Farming-dale*
Terrain: *Mostly flat*
Traffic: *Light to moderate*
Round-trip distance pedaled: *26.1 miles*
Highlights: *Allaire State Park and Village, Manasquan River, fishing, bird-watching*

Though the roar of the blast furnace can no longer be heard, Allaire Village stands as a reminder of the successful bog-iron industry in this area over 140 years ago. Allaire Village, where this trip begins, originally housed a sawmill operation in 1750; it was purchased by James Peter Allaire in 1822 for the supply of bog iron to operate his steamboat engine works in New York. Allaire was already a successful man, having built the cylinder for the SS *Savannah,* the first steam vessel to cross the Atlantic, in 1819.

With Allaire's expertise, the bog-iron works flourished; his village housed approximately 500 workers and their families. Craftspeople included molders, ware cleaners, carpenters, pattern makers, wheelwrights, millers, teamsters, stage drivers, grooms, and harness makers. Stoves, screws, pipe, hand irons, pots, and kettles were a few of the articles manufactured here.

Spend a while taking a self-guided walk through the village for a look at the restored row houses, formerly workers' homes; the millpond, fed by a stream named Mill Run and built to hold water that served as a source of power for the mill located along the streambank; and an old wooden farmhouse dating from the 1700s, used by the ironworks' manager. The Episcopal church that Allaire built for the community is unusual, for not only is the steeple situated over the pulpit, but also

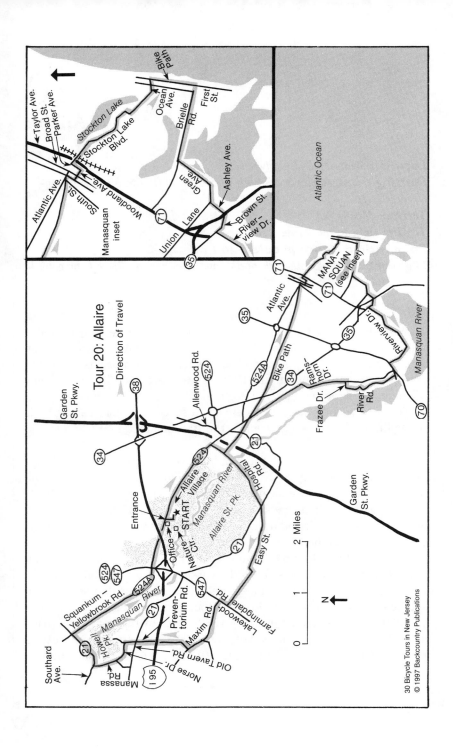

Tour 20: Allaire

Direction of Travel

30 Bicycle Tours in New Jersey
© 1997 Backcountry Publications

Take time to explore Allaire Village. In days long gone, 500 workers and their families lived in row houses such as these.

worshipers were not required to pay pew rents. Today many wedding ceremonies take place in the church.

The bog-iron industry declined as hardrock iron ore and anthracite were discovered in Pennsylvania around 1846, and although Allaire's son stayed on for four decades longer, people left the village, and it slowly decayed. Thankfully, the state has restored it, and today you can see the beehive-shaped blast furnace, watch demonstrations at the blacksmith shop, or limber up on one of the short, interesting trails within the park. You may wish to camp overnight, or longer, inside the park. Call 732-938-2253 (village) or 732-938-2371 (park) for further information. (The village is open daily; fee for parking from Memorial Day to Labor Day.)

Park in the Allaire Village parking lot; pedal to the parking lot exit, and reset your odometer when you reach Route 524.

0.0 *RIGHT onto Route 524 east.*

You might be here in time to see the steam locomotive pass by. Rides are available during summer months.

Just before climbing a gentle hill you'll see the lush green lawn of the Spring Meadow Golf Course, run by the state of New Jersey.

1.4 RIGHT onto Hospital Road.

There's a horse farm on this corner; if you have a spare carrot, you won't have to look far to share it.

1.7 LEFT onto the (unmarked) bicycle path, known as the Edgar Felix Bicycle Path and identified by a CLOSED TO MOTORIZED TRAFFIC sign.

Although power lines along this narrow, slightly rough road are unsightly, the surroundings are pleasant. Almost immediately on entering, you'll come to a small pond frequented by fishermen. Pine trees, rhododendron, and mountain laurel abound along this former rail line, partially obscuring houses set back from the path.

5.1 LEFT at the end of the bike trail in the Borough of Manasquan and an immediate RIGHT onto Atlantic Avenue.

Drinks and a rest room are available at the gas station.

5.4 RIGHT onto Broad Street and an immediate LEFT onto (unmarked) Woodland Avenue.

5.5 LEFT onto Parker Avenue.

Follow the road as it turns right. Continue straight across Taylor Avenue and the railroad tracks. The street name changes to Stockton Lake Boulevard. If you need food or drink, there's a restaurant on this corner and a soda machine at the liquor store.

Stockton Lake, to your left, is a good place to sit and have a snack while watching visiting mallards, egrets, and Canada geese. The National Guard Training Center is on the opposite side of the lake.

The road turns sharply right into North Potter.

6.3 First LEFT on Ocean Avenue, continuing straight to the ocean.

6.7 RIGHT on the paved ocean path.

Biking is permitted from October to May, but from June to September bicycles are allowed only between 6 and 9 AM. During restricted periods, use First Street.

The white sand and blue ocean are a refreshing change of scenery in spite of the tacky amusement section and refreshment stands on the right.

7.1 RIGHT onto Brielle Road (at the rest rooms on the beach).

The marina makes an interesting stop, but be prepared for stiff winds while crossing the drawbridge.

7.7 LEFT immediately after the drawbridge onto (unmarked) Green Avenue.

8.3 RIGHT onto Union Lane, then the first LEFT onto Ashley Avenue.

8.6 RIGHT onto Brown Street.

8.7 LEFT onto Riverview Drive.

During springtime, this residential neighborhood is ablaze with cherry, crab apple, and dogwood trees. As you pedal along the slightly hilly terrain, you'll pass a golf course, a pond, and many more impressive trees, including magnolias and Japanese maples.

10.3 LEFT onto Highway 70; then an immediate RIGHT at the fork in the road before the gas station.

10.6 RIGHT onto River Road.

The Manasquan River, on the left, was a favorite of the Lenni-Lenape. They named it the Manatahasquakan, meaning the place where they left their squaws while gathering shellfish at the ocean. They used the tall, straight tulip trees that still grow in these woods today for their canoes. Upstream, the river is known for its tasty trout.

Continue straight through this lovely residential neighborhood. Just before the road ends, look for an unusual house on the left and see if you can figure out what it represents. I'm still puzzled.

11.8 RIGHT at the end of River Road onto (unmarked) Frazee Drive.

11.9 LEFT onto Ramshorn Drive.

14.1 LEFT onto the bike path.

If you come to the stop sign at the Allenwood Road junction (opposite the Allenwood Grange building), you've gone too far; turn back and find the bicycle trail under the power lines. Or if you want a drink or snack, you can visit the Allenwood General Store before returning to the bike path.

14.8 LEFT onto Hospital Road.

This is another opportunity to watch the horses as they graze in the pasture if you missed them on the way out. Continue straight as Hospital Road becomes Easy Street.

18.2 *RIGHT at the T onto (unmarked) Lakewood-Farmingdale Road.*

18.4 *LEFT onto Maxim Road.*

19.6 *RIGHT onto Preventorium Road.*

Standing at the corner of Preventorium and Old Tavern Roads is the Ardena Public School #2, built in 1855. One of several hills in Monmouth County lies ahead.

20.8 *LEFT onto Norse Drive (at Police Headquarters).*

21.2 *RIGHT onto Manassa Road.*

21.7 *RIGHT onto Southard Avenue.*

22.4 *RIGHT onto Squankum-Yellowbrook Road.*

22.7 *RIGHT at the entrance to the Howell Park Golf Course.*

Pedal 0.2 mile to the iron bridge erected in 1852. Lock your bike and spend a while walking the path beneath the bridge alongside the Manasquan River. Spring is the best time of year to find an abundance of wildflowers here. Surprisingly, three different colors of violets can be found—purple, white, and yellow. In addition, there is the beautiful trout lily—a small, trumpet-shaped yellow flower—and lots of green skunk cabbage poking up in the wet areas. If you smell it, you'll know instantly how it got its name. Although Native Americans ate skunk cabbage, the plant is poisonous unless boiled several times. One of the first wildflowers of the season, its bloom begins the end of February and magically the snow around it melts as it pops up. Other flora include the five-petaled pink spring beauty, Jack-in-the-pulpit, trillium, and marsh marigold. You also may be lucky enough to spot a harmless black racer or rat snake or the pine snake that's fond of hanging from tree limbs.

Fall is a good time to study the trees. One worth noting is the ironwood, recognizable any time of year by its smooth, tight bark of wavy and twisting blue and gray bands. Should you swing an ax at this tree, it would probably swing back at you because the bark is so tough.

When you've finished exploring, return to the park entrance.

23.1 RIGHT on Squankum-Yellowbrook Road.

The entrance to Allaire State Park is at 26.1 miles.

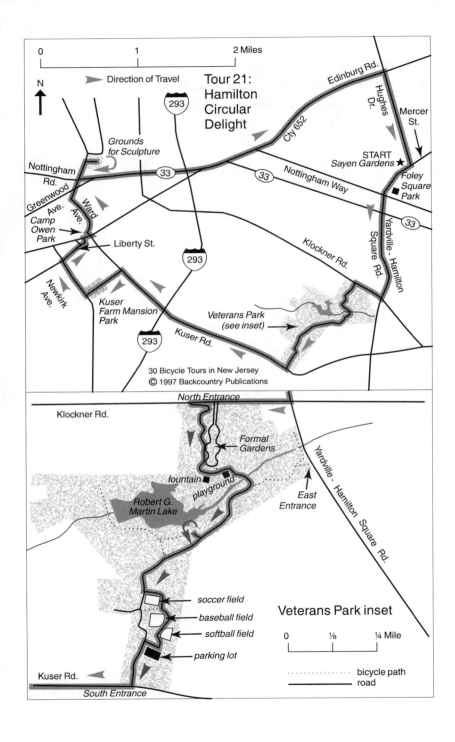

0   1   2 Miles

N

Direction of Travel

Tour 21: Hamilton Circular Delight

293

Edinburg Rd.

Hughes Dr.

Mercer St.

Grounds for Sculpture

Nottingham Rd.

Greenwood Ave.

Ward Ave.

Cty 652

START
Sayen Gardens ★

Foley Square Park

33

33

Nottingham Way

33

Camp Owen Park

Liberty St.

293

Klockner Rd.

Yardville - Hamilton Square Rd.

Newkirk Ave.

Kuser Farm Mansion Park

Veterans Park (see inset)

293

Kuser Rd.

30 Bicycle Tours in New Jersey
© 1997 Backcountry Publications

North Entrance

Klockner Rd.

Formal Gardens

fountain

playground

East Entrance

Yardville - Hamilton Square Rd.

Robert G. Martin Lake

soccer field

baseball field

softball field

parking lot

Veterans Park inset

0   ⅛   ¼ Mile

· · · · · · · · · · bicycle path
————— road

Kuser Rd.

South Entrance

21

Hamilton Circular Delight

Location: *Mercer County*
Starting point: *Sayen Gardens, Hughes Drive, Hamilton Township*
Terrain: *Flat*
Traffic: *Light*
Round-trip distance pedaled: *13.1 miles*
Highlights: *Gardens, including Sayen Gardens, Foley Square Park,*
Veterans Park, Kuser Farm Park, and Grounds for Sculpture, featuring
a wide variety of flowers and sculpture

This ride is delightful, especially during summer months when the flowers are in full bloom, and during fall when Mother Nature paints the trees in vibrant colors.

Start out as early as possible so that you have lots of time to admire each garden along the route. Although food and drink can be purchased in a number of places, bringing a picnic lunch not only saves money but also affords the opportunity to stop anywhere you may fancy when your stomach growls. For a real treat, wait until you reach Grounds for Sculpture; the outdoor café is a wonderful place to sit back, relax, and admire a pretty pond, exceptional view, and exquisite sculpture.

Park at Sayen Gardens, but before starting out, limber up by strolling through this magnificent picture-perfect garden, which features a dazzling array of flowers nearly year-round. Bicycles aren't allowed on the grounds, but can be locked in the parking lot.

0.0 RIGHT out of the garden entrance onto Hughes Drive.

0.2 RIGHT onto Mercer Street.

Foley Square Park, on the left at approximately 0.5 mile, is postage-stamp-sized but definitely worth a stop. If it's a hot day, you may want to dip your bandanna into the ornate fountain.

155

When you're ready to resume the tour, go straight through the intersection along Yardville–Hamilton Square Road and proceed past a farm on the right and housing developments on the left.

1.8 RIGHT onto Klockner Road.

2.1 LEFT into Veterans Park.

Located in the middle of Hamilton Township, this well-maintained park contains several sites of interest, including the John Abbott II farmhouse, which was raided by the British. Along the smooth bicycle trail are formal gardens, sculpture, a huge ornate water fountain surrounded by greenery and benches, athletic fields, a playground, public rest rooms, and a drinking fountain in case you have to fill your canteen.

2.4 RIGHT at the T.

2.6 RIGHT for a view of the Robert G. Martin Lake.

Just the sight and sound of ducks and geese is worth this short detour. If you have a fishing rod and license, you can try your luck.

2.8 LEFT away from the lake, bearing left at the V.

3.1 LEFT at the soccer field on the left and the parking lot on the right.

3.3 RIGHT at the parking lot.

3.5 RIGHT at the exit onto Kuser Road.

The Indian and Civil War Museums are on the right just before the exit.

5.6 LEFT into Kuser Farm Mansion Park.

USE CAUTION: There are a few speed bumps. Plan on stopping at the Kuser Farm Mansion and Gardens on the left at 6 miles. If the house is open, sign up for a tour. This 1888 Victorian-style mansion was the summer home of the Kuser family, who owned a New York City brewery. In addition to enjoying fresh country air, Kuser also engaged in many business ventures here, which included the movie industry and the manufacture of the Mercer automobile. On the tour, you'll see matched-grain oak paneling and ornate carving, lots of goodies from yesteryear, and an 18-foot curved projection screen used by Kuser and his closest friends to view movies he had invested in making before they appeared

Along the smooth bicycling trail within Veterans Park are formal gardens, sculpture, an ornate water fountain, and lots more.

before the general public. During summer months, free park concerts are held at the nearby gazebo; call 609-890-3630 for the schedule.

When you've finished exploring the park, bear right following Goldsmith Maid Memorial Road. At the curve sits a memorial honoring Goldsmith Maid, an American trotting horse that set a world record in 1874.

6.1 RIGHT at the two brick posts onto Newkirk Avenue.

6.5 RIGHT onto Liberty Street.

6.8 LEFT onto Ward Avenue.

Camp Owen Park is on the corner to the left. A huge cemetery is ahead on the right.

8.0 RIGHT into the driveway for the Grounds for Sculpture.

This 22-acre sculpture park and museum, located on the former site of the New Jersey State Fair Grounds, is not to be missed. Impressive sculpture is scattered on gently rolling terrain consisting of open spaces, courtyards, gardens, and pools. Continually changing exhibitions of monumental to smaller-scale sculpture by internationally known artists who work in many different media, including metal, wood, concrete, and stone, are held here throughout the year, while the spectacular glass-enclosed museum, reconstructed from an original fairgrounds building and now functioning as the entrance to the sculpture park, also houses dynamic contemporary art. (Hours vary; call 609-586-0616; fee.)

When you're ready to resume the tour, turn left back at the entrance onto Ward Avenue.

8.5 LEFT at the first traffic light, onto Nottingham Road.

8.6 Jog LEFT onto Greenwood Avenue.

Passing the cemetery again, you'll now be riding on a street with lots of small businesses. At 9.3 miles the name changes to Route 33.

10.1 Bear LEFT onto County Road 652.

This road shortly bears right, changing to Edinburg Road at 10.4 miles—a pretty, residential two-lane street with trees bordering the shoulder.

12.1 RIGHT onto Hughes Drive.

This wide, residential street is lined with trees and pretty lawns.

13.1 RETURN to Sayen Gardens, the starting point.

SOUTHERN NEW JERSEY

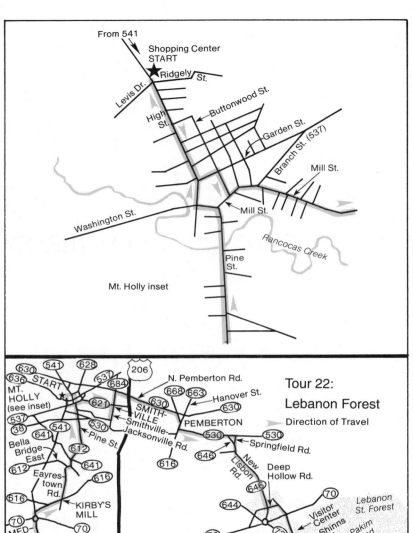

From 541

Shopping Center
START

Ridgely St.

Levis Dr.

High St.

Buttonwood St.

Garden St.

Branch St. (537)

Mill St.

Washington St.

Mill St.

Rancocas Creek

Pine St.

Mt. Holly inset

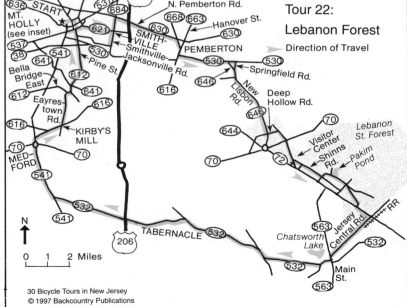

630 541 628 206 N. Pemberton Rd.

636 START 537 684 668 663 Hanover St.

MT. HOLLY (see inset) 621 SMITH-VILLE 630 530

537 530 Smithville- PEMBERTON

38 541 Jacksonville Rd. 530 530

641 Pine St. 616 646 Springfield Rd.

Bella Bridge East 612 New Lisbon Rd. Deep Hollow Rd.

612 641 616 646 70 Lebanon St. Forest

Eayres-town Rd. 644 Visitor Center Pakim Pond

616 KIRBY'S MILL 72 Shinns Rd.

70 70 70

MED-FORD

541

532

N 541 532 Jersey Central Rd. RR

0 1 2 Miles 206 TABERNACLE 532 Chatsworth Lake 563 532

532 Main St.

563

Tour 22:

Lebanon Forest

Direction of Travel

30 Bicycle Tours in New Jersey
© 1997 Backcountry Publications

22
Lebanon Forest

Location: *Burlington County*
Starting point: *Shopping center, High Street, Mount Holly*
Terrain: *Flat*
Traffic: *Light to moderate*
Round-trip distance pedaled: *52.9 miles*
Highlights: *Historic Mount Holly and Smithville, Pine Barrens, swimming, fishing*

A visit to this quiet section of Burlington County will make you feel as though you've stepped back in time. The trip begins in the historic town of Mount Holly, settled by Quakers from Yorkshire and London in the 17th century.

After pedaling past well-preserved buildings in Mount Holly, you continue on to Smithville, former home of the unique "Bicycle Railway," before entering the Pine Barrens and the tranquil Lebanon State Forest.

Park at the shopping center on the east side of High Street just north of the intersection with Levis Drive and Ridgely Street. If you're coming from I-295 or the New Jersey Turnpike (exit 5), take Route 541 South and make a left onto High Street. The shopping center is on your left. Pedal to the intersection of High Street and Levis Drive, resetting your odometer at this point.

0.0 STRAIGHT (south) on High Street.

High Street, in the oldest section of town, is lined with stately Georgian, Federal, and Carpenter Gothic houses. Stop in at the Mount Holly Visitor Center (at 0.4 mile on your left) if you want a map of local historic sites, such as the Prison Museum at 128 High Street. Built in 1810, this prison and workhouse was the first

The Burlington County Court House, dating back to 1796, is reputed to be
one of the finest examples of Colonial architecture in the nation.

fireproof building erected in the United States and, until 1965, the oldest prison in continuous use in America. Free tours are conducted from April through November on Wednesday and Saturday; call 609-265-5068 for hours, which vary. The interior design, including arched ceiling corridors, thick walls, and iron hardware, is very interesting but also depressing when you consider that prisoners lived in such crowded, cramped conditions.

Next door stands the Burlington County Court House (1796), reputed to be one of the finest examples of Colonial architecture in the nation. Farther down the street are the impressive tall spires that identify St. Andrew's Church.

0.7 LEFT onto Garden Street.

The Friends Meeting House (1775) on this corner was used for numerous state legislature meetings in 1779. Before that, British troops used it as a commissary; many of the butchers' cleaver marks are still visible on the benches.

0.8 RIGHT onto Buttonwood Street.

1.0 LEFT at the T onto Mill Street.

Hack's Canoe Rental, established in 1848 (opposite you on Rancocas Creek), was the first canoe rental business in the United States. Inside, three of the original canoes used are displayed.

Bear right at 1.2 miles, sticking with Mill Street as Route 537 veers to the left, after which the name changes to Mount Holly–Smithville Road. Traffic lightens as you enter open country.

3.0 RIGHT onto Smithville-Jacksonville Road.

The entrance to Smithville is at 3.3 miles. In 1865 Hezekiah Bradley Smith converted an abandoned thread mill here into a thriving machine manufacturing center. While the company produced a steam-powered bicycle and a kerosene-burning tricycle, one of its most lucrative items was the Star bicycle. It differed from all previous high-wheelers because it was built with a small guiding wheel in front of the large back wheel to ensure greater stability.

After Smith died, his associate built the Bicycle Railway to carry workers from Mount Holly to the factory. It resembled a rail fence; the rider simply sat between two wheels working the pedals up and down, instead of in a rotary motion, while a third wheel pressing against the bottom rail kept the bike in balance. At a top speed of 18 miles per hour, the rider reached the factory in minutes. The only problem was that riders had to pull off onto a siding when someone came from the opposite direction because a second rail was never built. The railway enjoyed great fame from 1892 to 1898, until the company declared bankruptcy.

3.3 LEFT (north) onto Smithville-Jacksonville Road, retracing your path.

4.2 RIGHT onto North Pemberton Road (Route 630).

This two-lane highway has a fairly wide shoulder with light traffic. Cross Route 206 at 4.9 miles. Many attractive farms may be seen along this stretch.

7.7 RIGHT following the sign for Pemberton.

8.1 RIGHT at the stop sign onto Hanover Street.

8.5 LEFT onto Route 530.

Leaving Pemberton, you encounter a narrow-shouldered section of road. Burlington County College comes up in approximately 2 miles.

11.4 RIGHT onto Springfield Road.

Grazing horses and lovely fields make pleasant vistas.

11.8 LEFT onto New Lisbon Road.

The fragrant aroma of pine marks your arrival at Lebanon State Forest, named for the Lebanon Glass Works established here in 1862. This vicinity was perfect for glassmaking because of an abundance of sand and wood for charcoal, but when the supply of wood became exhausted in 1867, the site was abandoned.

As you pedal down this long, quiet stretch of smooth, almost traffic-free road, it seems as though this part of the county hasn't been touched by time. Sand roads occasionally appear on either side, but unless you explore by foot, where they go will remain a mystery. The Pine Barrens appears awesome to some, but the area isn't really as barren as the name implies; the expression comes from colonial days when land was judged barren if it couldn't sustain traditional crops.

15.8 LEFT onto Deep Hollow Road.

Stick with this road as it turns sharply to the right at 16.5 miles; a pond soon appears on the right. This is a good spot to stretch, relax, have a drink, and perhaps soak your feet. After crossing Route 70, you'll come to Lebanon State Forest Visitor Center in about 0.75 mile. Rest rooms are available, along with maps and information. Don't sample the water here unless you're desperate; it has a high iron content and tastes terrible. If you want a bird's-eye view of the surrounding country, inquire about climbing the nearby fire tower before continuing on the same road.

17.9 LEFT at the T onto (unmarked) Shinns Road.

The journey is idyllic along this beautiful, peaceful stretch of road as the aroma of pine fills your nostrils.

19.8 LEFT at the T following the sign for Pakim Pond.

After a little more than 0.5 mile, look for the parking lot at Pakim Pond, a cozy waterhole developed from a former cranberry reservoir. The name Pakim is derived from a Lenni-Lenape word meaning "cranberry." Plan on spending a while taking in the peaceful scene, having lunch, going for a swim, or stretching your legs on the short trail circling the pond.

When you've finished with your rest stop, continue in the same direction as before, follow the road straight ahead through a campground area, and go around the locked gate when you come to it.

22.6 LEFT onto Route 72.

This is a main road; stay on the wide shoulder.

23.6 RIGHT onto (unmarked) Jersey Central Road, just before the railroad overpass.

Devoid of traffic, but full of potholes, this road follows through pines into Chatsworth.

26.6 LEFT onto Main Street, then immediately RIGHT on Route 532.

This is a l-o-n-g stretch, so settle down for pleasant riding through changing scenery along a flat, lightly traveled road sporting a wide shoulder most of the way. In about 0.5 mile you'll come to Chatsworth Lake, a scenic body of water surrounded by trees. The ride continues for several miles through pine forest before a second beautiful pond appears on the right side of the road where evergreens seem to grow right up to the water's edge. Farmland and a few private houses provide a change of pace before entering the village of Tabernacle at 36.3 miles. The cemetery here, deeded by William and Sarah Wilkens, is for residents of Tabernacle for as long as the "wheels of time shall not cease to roll."

Go straight after the stop sign at 36.4 miles, continuing on Route 532. Tabernacle is a good place to pick up food and drink. For a brief rest at a pretty brook, try Earl Jackson Memorial Park on your left at 41.5 miles.

41.7 RIGHT at the T onto Route 541.

Several stores here offer rest rooms and/or food. Stay on Route 541 as the road twists a bit. At Medford USE EXTREME CAUTION at the traffic circle across Route 70. Stay on Route 541 heading north.

45.0 RIGHT at the sign for Kirby's Mill.

Continue straight across the intersection at 45.6 miles on Church Road, Route 616 east. Kirby's Mill, a restoration, is a scenic place to stop and cast a line if you have time.

46.7 LEFT onto Eayrestown Road.

Huge farms are a delight to see along this stretch.

48.5 RIGHT at the T onto Bella Bridge East.

48.6 LEFT at the T onto Eayrestown Road.

Food, drink, and rest rooms are available at the intersection with Route 38. Continue straight ahead (you're now on Pine Street) back into the center of Mount Holly. Stop just before the end of this street at the firehouse on the right. Next to the modern structure stands the Relief Fire Company No. 1, the oldest continuously operated volunteer fire department in the country. In the days before fire engines, an alarm would bring volunteers to the station to get their leather fire buckets. Ask to see some of these ancient implements on display in the museum.

52.0 LEFT at the T onto Mill Street.

USE CAUTION: This is a dangerous intersection.

52.1 RIGHT at the traffic light onto High Street.

52.9 Reach the starting point.

23
Lakewood

Location: Ocean County
Starting point: Police Headquarters, Oak Avenue, Lakewood
Terrain: Flat
Traffic: Moderate
Round-trip distance pedaled: 36.1 miles
Highlights: Swimming, antiquing, bird-watching, beautiful woods

There is a humorous side to the merging of the old and new as communities quickly replace the farms and forests of northern Ocean County. For example, propped up against the front steps of an old farmhouse you may see a handwritten sign offering free horse manure—just across the street from a shiny new housing development.

Although you'll rarely experience solitude along these roads, you will, while inhaling the aroma of fragrant pine, capture a little of the remaining beauty that drew the wealthy to Lakewood in the era of the Gay Nineties. Many millionaires—including the Astors, Vanderbilts, Goulds, and Rockefellers—considered Ocean County's pine-scented air to be therapeutic and built their summer mansions around Lake Carasaljo. As the reputation of the area grew, visitors flocked here from miles around. Even today, during summer months Lakewood is still a very popular place for boating and swimming.

Park and begin at the Dover Township Police Headquarters parking lot on Oak Avenue, near the Bey-Lea Golf Course just north of Toms River. (Large groups should notify the officer in charge.) Reset your odometer at the parking lot exit nearest to the headquarters building.

0.0 LEFT (west) onto Oak Avenue.

0.1 LEFT onto Bay Avenue.

The Bey-Lea Municipal Golf Course is on your right.

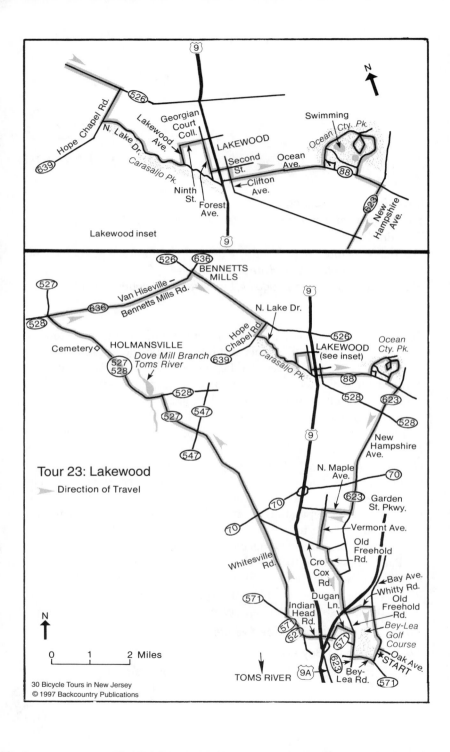

N

9

526

Hope Chapel Rd.

639

N. Lake Dr.

Georgian
Court
Coll.

Lakewood
Ave.

Carasaljo Pk.

LAKEWOOD

Second
St.

Ninth
St.

Clifton
Ave.

Forest
Ave.

Ocean
Ave.

Swimming

Ocean Cty. Pk.

88

623

New
Hampshire
Ave.

Lakewood inset

9

526   636

BENNETTS
MILLS

527

Van Hiseville –
Bennetts Mills Rd.

636

528

Cemetery

HOLMANSVILLE

527
528

Dove Mill Branch
Toms River

528

527

547

547

Hope Chapel Rd.

639

N. Lake Dr.

Carasaljo Pk.

9

526

LAKEWOOD
(see inset)

Ocean
Cty. Pk.

88

528

623

528

New
Hampshire
Ave.

N. Maple
Ave.

70

70

623

70

Garden
St. Pkwy.

Vermont Ave.

Old
Freehold
Rd.

Whitesville Rd.

Cro
Cox
Rd.

Dugan
Ln.

Bay Ave.

Whitty Rd.

Old
Freehold
Rd.

Bey-Lea
Golf
Course

Tour 23: Lakewood

Direction of Travel

N

0   1   2 Miles

30 Bicycle Tours in New Jersey
© 1997 Backcountry Publications

571

Indian
Head
Rd.

571
62

571

623

Oak Ave.

START

Bey-
Lea Rd.

571

TOMS RIVER

9A

0.4 RIGHT onto Bey-Lea Road, Route 571.

As you pedal along the edge of the golf course, enjoy the pleasant vista of green grass and tall border trees.

0.9 RIGHT onto Old Freehold Road.

1.5 LEFT onto Dugan Lane.

After passing a residential neighborhood, the road bends and runs parallel to the Garden State Parkway. During summer months you'll probably be pedaling faster than the cars!

2.3 RIGHT at the T onto Indian Head Road.

Go under the parkway and cross Route 9. Watch out for some interesting obstacles: This wide, busy road is frequented by Canada geese nearly year-round. A pond is on your right at 2.8 miles.

3.7 RIGHT onto Whitesville Road, Route 527.

Here you'll see housing developments as well as remnants of farms and country stores. Woodchucks love to cross this smooth, wide-shouldered road. After crossing Route 70, at 6.4 miles you'll travel through a wooded area and will pass an antiques shop and country store. There is also a small pond along this stretch.

10.4 LEFT at the T, continuing on Route 527.

The pond at 10.7 miles is a perfect place for a break. This section of the road, which passes by a small dam holding back the Dove Mill Branch of the Toms River, has a broad shoulder. At 12.7 miles you'll come to the Holmanville Cemetery, founded in 1845.

14.2 RIGHT onto (unmarked) Van Hiseville–Bennetts Mills Road, following the sign for Freehold.

After this intersection, just past the Jackson First Aid Station, is the start of a pleasant, uncrowded stretch offering fine country cycling and an exciting long downhill pass before entering the town of Bennetts Mills. If you didn't take a break at the last pond, there is another opportunity at 17.8 miles.

18.0 RIGHT onto Route 526.

Food, drink, and rest rooms are available here. USE CAUTION: The road widens to four lanes with lots of traffic and no shoulder.

20.3 RIGHT onto Hope Chapel Road.

A chapel and cemetery are on the right at 20.5 miles.

20.8 LEFT onto North Lake Drive.

Carasaljo Park, on the right, has magnificent stands of oak, pine, hemlock, and cedar. On your left there are huge houses sporting beautifully landscaped lawns. In about 1 mile you'll come to Lake Carasaljo, named by iron master Joseph W. Brick for his daughters, Carrie, Sally, and Josephine. Stop at 22.0 miles for a look at the sculpture gardens in Georgian Court College, on the left.

22.3 LEFT onto Lakewood Avenue.

These are the grounds of Georgian Court College, a private college. The 200-acre estate, originally owned by New York financier George J. Gould, is exquisite. Unfortunately, visitors aren't encouraged to tour the grounds except by appointment, but you can peek in and see quite a bit of the fountains, sunken gardens, and formal gardens.

22.5 RIGHT onto Ninth Street.

22.8 RIGHT onto Forest Avenue.

23.3 LEFT onto Second Street.

23.6 RIGHT onto Clifton Avenue.

Numerous opportunities to purchase food and drink are available here.

23.7 LEFT onto Main Street (Route 88).

The road name soon changes to Ocean Avenue. Hold on tight in this section; for about 1 mile you'll have to dodge sewer grates, holes, tar patches, and heavy traffic. Fortunately, the next stop makes up for the inconvenience.

24.9 LEFT into Ocean County Park.

Cyclists don't have to pay to enter this 323-acre recreational showplace donated by the heirs of John D. Rockefeller Sr., who once lived on these grounds. The park has more than 150 species of trees and shrubs, plus a herd of deer. At one time it was used as the spring training headquarters for the New York Giants baseball team.

Ocean County Park has delightful cycling trails through wooded areas and a beach and ponds for swimming.

Follow the main park road to the swimming area at 25.4 miles. This safe, sandy beach, nestled in the pines, is a delight during summer months.

25.7 RIGHT *between wooden posts onto the bicycle path.*

This unmarked bicycling path, opposite a long, low building, leads to a beautiful small pond that's an ideal place to sit, relax, have lunch, or identify birds alighting on tree branches.

25.9 LEFT, *following the bicycle path along the pond's edge.*

Stay on the path; it turns left less than 0.1 mile after the pond and follows past the Police Academy located on the right.

26.2 RIGHT *between wooden posts onto the park road.*

As you circle through the park, you'll pass tennis courts, a well-stocked lake, and large playing fields.

27.0 LEFT *onto Ocean Avenue.*

27.4 RIGHT *at the traffic light onto New Hampshire Avenue.*

Traffic is moderate along this smooth road.

30.8 RIGHT onto North Maple Avenue.

You may wish to stop and rest at this horse farm for a while. Enjoy the bucolic atmosphere in the midst of a populated area.

31.4 LEFT at the stop sign onto Vermont Avenue.

32.3 LEFT onto Cox Cro Road.

32.5 RIGHT onto Old Freehold Road.

The shoulder is wide on this section. At 33.5 miles, bear right as New Hampshire Road joins in from the left.

34.2 LEFT on Whitty Road.

34.9 RIGHT at the T on Bay Avenue.

The Bey-Lea Golf Course is on the right.

36.0 LEFT on Oak Avenue.

36.1 ARRIVE at the parking lot.

24
Berkeley Island and Double Trouble

Location: *Ocean County*
Starting point: *Berkeley Island County Park, Brennan Concourse, Cedar Beach*
Terrain: *Flat*
Traffic: *Light, depending on season*
Round-trip distance pedaled: *21.1 miles*
Highlights: *Swimming, sunbathing, fishing*

This pleasant, leisurely cycling trip meanders through communities bordering Barnegat Bay and the Toms River before reaching Double Trouble State Park. You'll have the opportunity not only to observe boaters, swimmers, and sunbathers, but also to join them, depending on your inclination and the season.

Although the Jersey shore is overrun with vacationers during summer months, this route avoids most of the busy areas; spring, fall, and even a mild winter's day are ideal times to cycle this route.

Begin at Berkeley Island County Park, a small, scenic recreation area located on a 23-acre peninsula along Barnegat Bay. The bay offers excellent crabbing and fishing, as well as picnic tables and rest rooms. To reach the park, take Route 9 south of the municipality of Toms River, turn east at the traffic light on Butler Boulevard, and follow the signs. **Park** your car in the paved parking area, resetting your bicycle odometer when you reach the entrance to the parking lot.

0.0 STRAIGHT *ahead (west) on park entrance road (Brennan Concourse).*

0.6 RIGHT *onto South Bayview Avenue.*

At 1.6 miles, stay right at the fork. Listen closely; the soft sounds

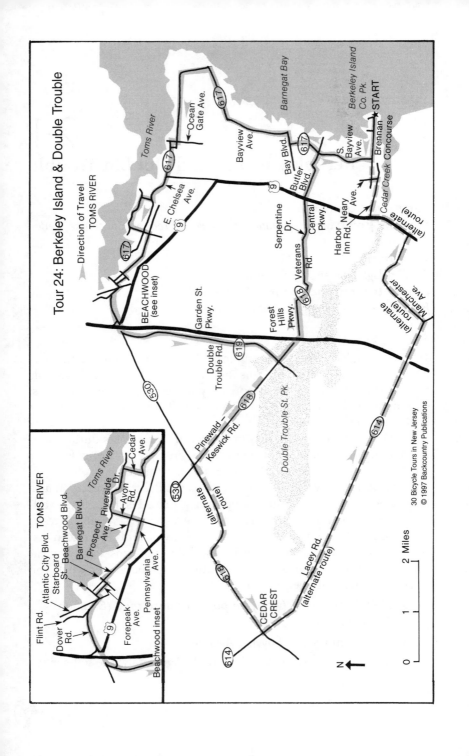

Tour 24: Berkeley Island & Double Trouble

Direction of Travel
TOMS RIVER

Barnegat Bay

Toms River

Berkeley Island
Co. Pk.

617

Ocean Gate Ave.

617

Bayview Ave.

617

Bay Blvd.

617

S. Bayview Ave.

Brennan
Concourse

START

Butler Blvd.

617

Cedar Creek

E. Chelsea Ave.

9

Serpentine Dr.

Central Pkwy.

Harbor Inn Rd.

Neary Ave.

(alternate route)

BEACHWOOD
(see inset)

Veterans Rd.

618

(alternate route)

Manchester Ave.

Garden St. Pkwy.

Forest Hills Pkwy.

Double Trouble Rd.

619

530

Double Trouble St. Pk.

Pinewald — Keswick Rd.

618

530 (alternate route)

614

618

CEDAR CREST

Lacey Rd.

614

(alternate route)

30 Bicycle Tours in New Jersey
© 1997 Backcountry Publications

N

0   1   2 Miles

Beachwood inset

TOMS RIVER

Toms River

Cedar Ave.

Atlantic City Blvd.

Starboard St.

Beachwood Blvd.

Barnegat Blvd.

Riverside Dr.

Prospect Ave.

Avon Rd.

Flint Rd.

Dover Rd.

9

Forepeak Ave.

Pennsylvania Ave.

you'll hear in this area are from the huge stands of marsh grasses as they rub against each other in the breeze.

2.4 RIGHT onto Bay Boulevard.

This wide road has a good shoulder edged with more marsh grasses and healthy pine trees.

2.5 LEFT onto Bayview Avenue.

If you like, use the restaurant on the corner for a pit stop or a quick bite before proceeding. You'll pass through a neighborhood recently converted from former marshland. The lawns are worth a look; some homeowners are using their ingenuity by decorating with driftwood, rock, or lush beds of marsh grass. The lagoons are man-made, and most houses at the water's edge are fortunate to have boat slips. Boat rental places along this stretch usually have soda machines and rest rooms.

6.7 RIGHT onto Ocean Gate Avenue.

6.8 LEFT onto East Chelsea Avenue, which turns into Prospect Avenue.

At about 6.9 miles you'll find a nice spot to rest: A large grassy area is on the left, and a small stream faces an inlet to the right.

8.1 RIGHT onto Cedar Avenue.

8.4 LEFT onto Riverside Drive, at the edge of the Toms River.

The route follows the river for a little more than 0.5 mile. You may wish to stop for a view of sail- and powerboats, or to take a swim or walk out onto the pier at 8.9 miles to stretch your legs.

9.0 LEFT onto Avon Road.

9.5 RIGHT onto Pennsylvania Avenue, which changes to Barnegat Boulevard.

10.4 LEFT at the T onto Beachwood Boulevard.

10.5 RIGHT onto Forepeak Avenue.

10.7 LEFT at the T onto Starboard Street.

10.8 RIGHT onto Atlantic City Boulevard. Make an immediate LEFT, then an immediate RIGHT onto Flint Road.

11.0 LEFT onto Dover Road.

When the sawmill at Double Trouble State Park is open, you'll see this circular saw dating from 1883. It's capable of cutting 1000 shingles an hour.

11.7 LEFT onto Double Trouble Road.

Along this lightly traveled road are lovely stands of pine, oak, and sassafras. Although the road parallels the Garden State Parkway, you'll feel far from civilization.

At 15.0 miles you'll come to the entrance to Double Trouble State Park. The origin of the park's name remains a mystery. A naturalist with the Ocean County Parks System reports that it was named Double Trouble by a preacher and his wife in the 1840s after muskrats dug holes in their dam twice in one week. Architectural historians, however, recently attributed the name to an 18th-century sawmill owner who, after being told that spring floods had washed out the dam above his mill for the second time in two days, remarked, "Now we have double trouble!"

If you're feeling adventurous and don't mind cycling along sand roads, take some time to explore the park. Head over to the circa-1765 sawmill, and if it's in operation, ask permission to stay and watch it work. You'll learn how complicated it is to produce cedar shingles from logs—especially when 1000 shingles an hour are cut using a machine built in 1883! Outside the mill are remnants of a former logging village dating to 1812, when white cedar was logged from surrounding swamps for building ships. After the swamps were cleared, the land was used for cranberry production.

15.0 LEFT (east) onto Pinewald-Keswick Road at the entrance to Double Trouble State Park.

The route from this point leads directly back to Berkeley Island County Park. For a longer trip (by about 16 miles), see the alternate route below.

Pinewalk-Keswick Road meanders, changing names several times (Forest Hills Parkway, Veterans, Serpentine, Central Parkway), and finally turns into Butler Boulevard where it crosses Route 9 (at 18.5 miles) at a traffic light.

19.4 RIGHT onto (unmarked) South Bayview Avenue at the sign for Berkeley Island Park.

20.5 LEFT onto Brennan Concourse.

21.1 ARRIVE at starting point.

ALTERNATE ROUTE: If you wish to take the alternate route,

which adds about 16 miles, make a RIGHT turn at Pinewald-Keswick Road at the entrance to Double Trouble State Park; follow Route 618 to Cedar Crest, and make a LEFT onto Lacey Road (Route 614). After crossing the Garden State Parkway, make a LEFT onto Manchester Avenue, another LEFT onto Route 9, and a RIGHT onto Harbor Inn Road. A LEFT onto Neary Avenue and a RIGHT onto Brennan Concourse will take you back to Berkeley Island Park.

25
Island Beach State Park

Location: Ocean County
Starting point: Island Beach State Park entrance gate, Central Avenue, Seaside Park
Terrain: Flat
Traffic: Light from Labor Day through Memorial Day
Round-trip distance pedaled: 17.4 miles
Highlights: Nature museum, interpretive center, nature trails, bird-watching, swimming, Barnegat Lighthouse, natural dunes and vegetation

If I haven't been bicycling for a while, I usually get back into shape by taking this trip because it's flat, easy, and delightful year-round. Bring a bathing suit during warm weather so that you can cool off in the ocean after the ride. It's also great spending some time on the beautiful sand beach at any time of year, listening to the surf or watching the seagulls perform their acrobatic dances while in flight.

One of the few natural barrier beaches remaining on the Atlantic Coast, Island Beach State Park, a 10-mile white sand strip, boasts one of the largest osprey colonies in the state. In addition, over 240 bird species have been sighted here, including the peregrine falcon, brown pelican, blue heron, and the endangered piping plover, least tern, and black skimmer. Most likely you'll also encounter a red fox or two along the ride, since they're common in this area.

According to park officials, about 3000 acres of Island Beach were once part of an island created in 1750 when the sea opened an inlet between the ocean and Barnegat Bay near the northern end of the park area. Then known as Cranberry Inlet, it was a highly regarded shipping area in Barnegat Bay used by the New Jersey Privateers, a group sanctioned by the government to raid British ships.

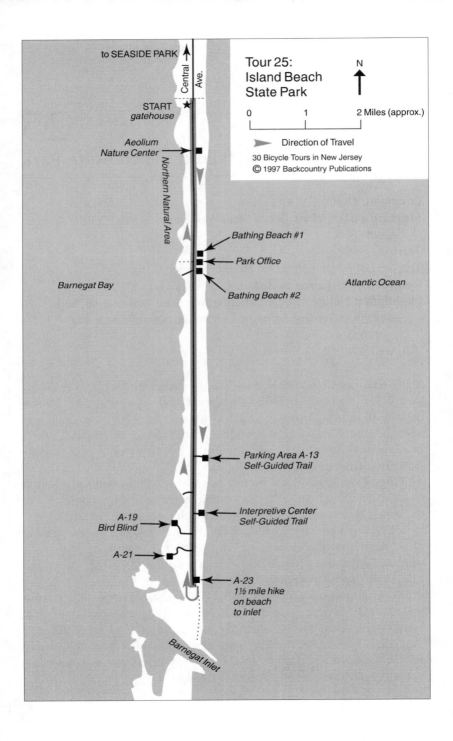

to SEASIDE PARK

Central Ave.

START
gatehouse

Tour 25:
Island Beach
State Park

N

0   1   2 Miles (approx.)

Direction of Travel

30 Bicycle Tours in New Jersey
© 1997 Backcountry Publications

Aeolium
Nature Center

Northern Natural Area

Bathing Beach #1

Park Office

Barnegat Bay

Atlantic Ocean

Bathing Beach #2

Parking Area A-13
Self-Guided Trail

Interpretive Center
Self-Guided Trail

A-19
Bird Blind

A-21

A-23
1½ mile hike
on beach
to inlet

Barnegat Inlet

Pirates had various methods of luring vessels ashore. These included the use of false lights that simulated a ship at sail or at anchor, flashing false signals from a lighthouse, and tying a lantern onto an animal's back. Someone would then lead the animal along the dunes parallel to the coast so that the light would appear to be another vessel to an unsuspecting captain, who, in turn, would steer his vessel toward the light. Once it ran aground, the vessel fell easy prey to the pirates.

Henry Phipps, visualizing the area as a beach resort for the upper class, purchased Island Beach in 1926. However, he died before his dream came true. Thankfully, when Francis Freeman took over the estate, he preserved the natural beauty of Island Beach by allowing only certain visitors to enter, provided they followed his rules of "no berry picking, dune destruction, littering, and reckless plundering of natural resources." The few lucky visitors he allowed in for day use were able to hunt, fish, and stroll.

Everything changed in the 1940s: The War Department declared the island a restricted area and forced everyone to leave so that the Army and Johns Hopkins University could work here on anti-aircraft rocketry. Amazingly, in 1945 they were successful in launching a supersonic ram-jet rocket that traveled over 9 miles at one-and-a-half times the speed of sound.

Fortunately, in 1953 the state and various fishermen's groups raised $2.75 million to purchase the property from the Phipps estate, ensuring that the national beauty of Island Beach would be preserved and used by everyone. Despite the fact that over 800,000 visitors use the park each year, it looks today much as it did during the 1700s.

It's best to **park** your car inside the park, but if you want to avoid the entry fee, space is usually available very early in the morning outside the park entrance. If you choose to park outside, you'll pass many small bungalows that are summer rentals, along with seafood restaurants.

Gatehouse rest rooms are open 24 hours daily, and rest rooms at the office 9–3. A year-round heated facility can be found at the A-6/7 lots 24 hours daily. If you visit during summer and want to explore the side trails, remember to take insect repellent to avoid mosquito bites.

0.0 Head STRAIGHT past the toll gate booth on your left.

You'll immediately experience a feeling of solitude while taking in the wonderful fresh sea-air aroma. The bay is to the right, as are tall phragmites with large, fluffy plumes waving in the slightest breeze. The ocean and beach are to the left, along with lovely pine and cedar trees, which add a touch of warmth to the scene during winter months.

Winter is particularly peaceful here and a good time to treasure hunt, but remember not to take live specimens. An occasional starfish can be found on the beach, as well as egg cases from long skates and purple sea urchins. At low tide, thousands of barnacles can be seen clinging to the rocks, and if you dig into the sand at the water's edge, you may find sand crabs. In late spring horseshoe crabs are strewn all over the beach; that's when they arrive to lay eggs in the shallow water.

At 0.7 mile you'll pass US Life Saving Service station #110, now used as a maintenance building.

1.5 STOP here for a visit to the Aeolium.

Lock your bike to one of the racks and spend some time in this tiny but excellent interpretive nature center, named after the Greek god of the wind. You'll learn about the fauna and flora of a barrier island and enjoy hands-on exhibits and interesting slide presentations on topics related to Island Beach. This is also the starting point for naturalist-conducted tours held during summer months; call 732-793-0506 for specific hours. Also consider exploring the easy 0.8-mile self-guided nature trail that starts from behind the building and leads through dunes and thicket. Signs describing the vegetation and dune formations are posted, but be careful: Poison ivy thrives here, as it does in the rest of the park. A path across the road leads to Barnegat Bay.

3.5 EXIT the Northern Natural Area, continuing straight ahead.

The dunes on the left are outstanding. If you'd like to take a dip in the ocean, an entrance to bathing beach #1 is straight ahead and on the left in 0.3 mile.

3.7 LEFT for the park office, which is handicapped accessible.

Stop in to have questions answered, pick up informative brochures on the area, view wayside exhibits, or use the rest rooms. Bathing beach #2 is just ahead on the left, and at area A-7 you'll find a boardwalk leading to the ocean.

Stretch your legs along the beautiful sand beach for a look at
the impressive Barnegat Lighthouse, built in 1858.

4.0 Continue STRAIGHT.

During summer months, you may encounter some traffic as people head to the beach parking areas. There are many interesting stops along the way worth exploring; the well-marked parking areas are on the left side of the road.

At parking area A-13, a short, self-guiding trail leads to the ocean. Search for cranberries growing in the freshwater wetlands along the way and, if you're here in September, check out the ripe beach plums.

Parking area A-17 leads to the bay and a Coast Guard station. For a 0.4-mile leg stretch leading to a bird observation blind, park at A-19. The walkway, which goes past lots of junipers and hollies, begins on the right side of the road heading toward the bay. Ospreys and waterfowl can be observed close by. When you're ready to resume the tour, continue straight ahead, pedaling past a boat ramp area on your right.

At the A-21 parking area, a path leads to the bay, where canoe and kayak tours are scheduled during summer months.

8.7 STOP at the end of the road and PARK at A-23.

Don't miss this opportunity to walk along the beautiful sand beach. For a look at the impressive Barnegat Lighthouse, built in 1858, turn right and continue walking. On the way, with salt spray from breaking waves hitting your face, note the flora in the area. The first 6 inches of sand are bone dry, supporting only those plants that can tolerate such conditions. The dune grass, which stabilizes the dunes, sports pretty yellow flowers in the spring. You'll also find black cherry in this dry area and the attractive prickly pear cactus, which produces a huge edible fruit that turns bright red when ripe. A few of the annuals that abound at the upper beach include sea rocket and seaside goldenrod, while the secondary dunes support lush American holly, red cedar, and magnolia. Rose hips, rich in vitamin C, as well as trumpet vine and beach plum, are also found here.

When you've finished taking in the sights, return the way you came to the starting point and your car.

26
Batsto

Location: *Atlantic and Burlington Counties*
Starting point: *Batsto Village, Wharton State Forest (off Route 542 west of the Garden State Parkway), Hammonton*
Terrain: *Mostly flat*
Traffic: *Very light*
Round-trip distance pedaled: *44.6 miles*
Highlights: *Batsto Village, historic Smithville, winery tour, Pine Barrens, scenic river*

This trip starts at Batsto Village where an iron furnace—which operated around the clock two centuries ago—played a key role in the industrial development of the United States by producing iron pots, kettles, and Dutch ovens. Later, when the American colonies struggled for independence from the British Crown, the furnace was used to make weapons for the Revolutionary Army.

According to a park brochure, "Batsto" is derived from the Swedish word *batstu,* meaning "bathing place." The village was founded in 1766 by Charles Read of Burlington, New Jersey, who was, according to park officials, "the most noted iron master in West Jersey prior to the Revolution. He built the Batsto Iron Works near the mouth of the Batsto River, the first known bog-iron furnace to be established here." During the War of 1812, the furnace was again used for warfare fittings, but by the mid-1830s the discovery of coal in Pennsylvania decreased the need for bog iron, and the village began to fail. Plan on spending an hour or two exploring the village before starting out. (Hours vary depending on the season; call 609-561-3262. Free except for parking fee charged weekends and holidays from Memorial Day through Labor Day; admission for mansion house tour.)

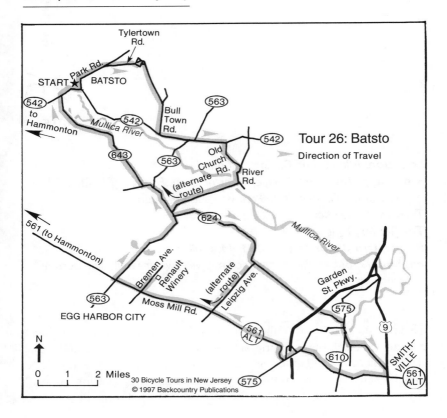

Tylertown Rd.

START ★ BATSTO

Park Rd.

542 to Hammonton

Mullica River

542

643

563

Old Church Rd.

Bull Town Rd.

563

(alternate route)

River Rd.

542

Tour 26: Batsto

Direction of Travel

561 (to Hammonton)

624

Bremen Ave.

Renault Winery

(alternate route)

Leipzig Ave.

Mullica River

Garden St. Pkwy.

563

Moss Mill Rd.

EGG HARBOR CITY

575

561 ALT

9

N

0 1 2 Miles

610

575

SMITH-VILLE

561 ALT

30 Bicycle Tours in New Jersey
© 1997 Backcountry Publications

The rest of the trip is equally pleasant. Most of the roads, with the exception of Route 643, have little traffic and provide solitude while pedaling. The quiet beauty of the Pine Barrens is a refreshing change from crowds, and a couple of rewards on this trip are wine sampling at the Renault Winery and shopping at historic Smithville Village.

Pedal to the **parking** lot exit at Batsto Village and reset your odometer.

0.0 LEFT onto the (unnamed) park road.

The Batona Trail comes into view at 0.2 mile, and a fire tower is visible at 0.4 mile. The road is so quiet that all you'll hear is the whirl of the bicycle tires and birds chirping in overhead branches. The scent of pine trees is delightful. Although this road changes names several times, you won't notice it because of the lack of signs. It gradually curves around to the right.

5.1 LEFT at the T onto Route 542.

This road has some traffic and a wide shoulder. Snacks and drinks are available at a number of places.

7.4 RIGHT onto Old Church Road.

8.5 RIGHT at the T onto River Road.

At about 8.9 miles, you'll reach the Mullica River at a private boat launch. Named for Eric Mullica, who settled his Swedish colony on the shores of the river in 1697, the Mullica was the Native Americans' favorite oyster-gathering place. Today it's a hit with canoeists.

9.2 Follow the road across the bridge.

Fishing from the bridge is a favorite activity. Look for swamp grasses after crossing the bridge and for blue flag iris in springtime. Lush groves of pine trees shortly appear along this straight, smooth road.

11.9 LEFT at the T onto Route 563.

ALTERNATE ROUTE: To short-circuit this trip, go RIGHT instead and then follow directions at 38.3 miles (see map).

12.0 LEFT onto Route 624.

Maples, especially colorful during fall, line this long, usually traffic-free stretch.

ALTERNATE ROUTE: To shorten the trip by 10.8 miles, go RIGHT on Leipzig Avenue at 15.9 miles; then make a RIGHT onto Moss Mill Road (Alternate Route 561) after 2.3 miles. Follow directions at 31.5 miles (see map).

19.5 RIGHT at the T at the junction with Route 575. Continue straight ahead on what is now Route 610 East.

19.8 Cross the bridge, then bear LEFT following the sign to Smithville.

A side road comes off to the left at 20.6 miles. Bear right at this junction, following the main road.

22.0 RIGHT onto Route 9. This will immediately lead to Old Smithville on the right.

This is a pleasant area to stretch, watch the ducks, have some ice cream, or shop. An inn built in 1787 stands in the center of this restored village that includes numerous Early American village shops and buildings, a gristmill, and a general store. (Open daily; free.) When you're through exploring, return to the Route 9 entrance.

22.0 Continue south on Route 9.

22.1 RIGHT turn at the first intersection onto Alternate Route 561, Moss Mill Road.

The Pomona golf course provides lush greenery along the way.

31.5 RIGHT onto Bremen Avenue at the sign for Renault Winery.

32.2 RIGHT at the entrance to Renault Winery. Walk your bike along the gravel driveway to the winery.

Lock your bicycle to a post in the parking lot and take some time to explore the winery, reputed to be the oldest continuously operated vineyard in the United States. It was founded in the late 19th century by master winemaker Louis Nicholas Renault, a native of Rheims, France. Renault found the soil of south Jersey similar to that of certain vineyards in France and began producing champagne in 1870. While Prohibition spelled the end for wineries, this one prospered thanks to its new product, Renault Tonic. People rushed to their drugstore to purchase this elixir, advertised as a youth potion and backache remedy—although it was actually a wine in disguise. Cleverly, the company didn't use the word "wine" anywhere on the front label, but on the back label it wrote a simple message: "Caution: Do not refrigerate this tonic as it will turn into wine."

Today the Milza family owns the winery, and for one dollar you can take a nice break and sample some of the champagnes and wines, including Cold Duck, cabernet sauvignon, and others. You can also tour the Glass Museum, where over 300 champagne glasses are displayed, and look at old wine presses and antique bottling machinery in an Italianate Spanish-style courtyard.

Batsto Village offers a look at an old iron furnace, a chance to cast off in the water, and a look at historic buildings.

When you're through touring the winery, continue to Bremen Avenue, turn left, and return to the junction with Moss Mill Road.

33.1 RIGHT onto Moss Mill Road (Alternate Route 561 north).

33.9 RIGHT onto Route 563.

At 35.4 miles you'll see bodies of water on both sides of the road and a campground on the right.

38.3 Continue STRAIGHT ahead onto Route 643 at the junction of Routes 563 and 643.

The scenic Mullica River is adjacent to the right side of the road at 40.9 miles.

43.3 RIGHT onto Route 542.

44.2 LEFT at the entrance to Batsto area.

44.6 ARRIVE at the entrance to the Batsto parking lot.

Forsythe Wildlife Refuge Roundabout

Location: *Atlantic County*
Starting point: *Edwin B. Forsythe National Wildlife Refuge, off Route 9 South, Oceanville*
Terrain: *Flat*
Traffic: *Light*
Round-trip distance pedaled: *8 miles*
Highlights: *Atlantic Flyway route, cordgrass and salt grass tidal marsh, abundant wildlife*

You don't have to be a bird lover to enjoy the sights and sounds along this short, thrilling route, for the 36,000-acre Edwin B. Forsythe National Wildlife Refuge is wonderful year-round. Plan on spending a couple of hours riding and stopping along this 8-mile trail. Provided you don't disturb the wildlife, you can stop wherever you fancy to admire the birds, take photographs, or simply listen to the constant chatter surrounding you. While bicycling in the refuge, it's easy to forget that Atlantic City's casinos are so near. However, they're visible along the horizon.

During summer visits, be sure to douse yourself with ample insect repellent. Despite having to brave the mosquitoes, you'll be rewarded by the sight of hundreds of flowers, including wisteria vines ablaze with purple flowers at the entrance, Japanese honeysuckle scattered here and there, and open fields shimmering with large yellow black-eyed Susans.

Bring food and drink; a picnic area is available, as are rest rooms, drinking water, and a reporting station for birders. A small fee is charged for parking at the refuge unless you hold a Golden Age Pass; hours are from sunrise to sunset; 609-652-1665. After **parking** your car, obtain a self-guiding wildlife guide from the visitors building, read the list of cur-

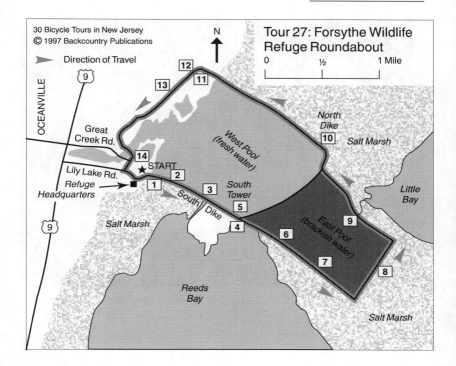

30 Bicycle Tours in New Jersey
© 1997 Backcountry Publications

N

Tour 27: Forsythe Wildlife Refuge Roundabout

0   ½   1 Mile

Direction of Travel

OCEANVILLE

Great Creek Rd.

Lily Lake Rd.

Refuge Headquarters

START

South Dike

South Tower

West Pool (fresh water)

North Dike

Salt Marsh

Little Bay

East Pool (brackish water)

Salt Marsh

Salt Marsh

Reeds Bay

rent sightings, and head to the fee booth.

0.0 Go STRAIGHT from the fee booth.

The scene is quite impressive the moment you enter the refuge. On the right at 0.1 mile is the Leeds Eco-Trail, a 0.5-mile nature trail that's well worth a stop to limber up. It's a mini-introduction to the refuge and a good place to spot raccoons, foxes, and opossums.

When you're ready to begin the tour, return to the main road, which goes over the South Dike. Constructed over an old railroad bed that once connected Brigantine Island to the mainland, it now serves as the southern wall of a dike system with a freshwater and a brackish pool; it's surrounded by a salt marsh on the right.

0.4 STOP for a look at the West Pool.

The 900-acre pool on the left is managed by water-control structures that permit the outflow of fresh water and prevent salt water on the bay side from entering. It attracts and supports a wide vari-

Cycling through the Forsythe Wildlife Refuge is a great way
to get into shape while spotting hundreds of birds.

ety of waterfowl, wading birds, and shorebirds that use the area
for resting, bathing, drinking, and feeding. During fall and spring
migrations you'll find freshwater-loving birds such as wood ducks
here; in fall and winter, you'll find huge flocks of Atlantic brant.

Continue, watching for ducks "tipping up" in the water as they
dunk to feed on aquatic plants. At Turtle Cove, the water level
fluctuates up to 2 feet twice each day as the tidal waters in the salt
marsh and Turtle Cove ebb and flow. During May and June, horseshoe crabs can be observed spawning at the cove, and during winter, brant can be observed picking up sand or grit that is retained
in their gizzards to grind up food.

1.0 LEFT to park at the South Tower.

This is a terrific spot to observe the variety of wetland habitats created by diking and water management. During spring and fall,
thousands of migrating waterbirds rest and feed in this area, and
in late fall and winter, flocks of Atlantic brant fly over the salt bays

while black ducks can be seen in the pools. The sight of tens of thousands of snow geese resting and feeding in the salt marsh and pools in November and early December is awesome.

1.5 LEFT to view the East Pool.

This 700-acre prime nesting area of gadwalls, shovelers, and ruddy ducks is a mixture of salt and fresh water. Over 3000 duck-lings are born here each year.

Look for blackened burn areas just ahead. Now sprouting new growth, these sections are intentionally burned by refuge man-agers to reduce the flammable plant debris accumulations on the pool edges and islands. Goslings start arriving here in May, and by mid-June ducklings can be seen.

Farther ahead at stop 10 you'll come to North Dike, an area that attracts many wading birds including the mute swan, one of the heaviest flying birds in the world. Adults often weigh up to 40 pounds.

3.0 STOP in this area for the sounds of the marsh.

This is a great spot to rest for a few moments, especially if you come between late April and September; that's when you'll hear the clattering call of the clapper rail, a salt marsh resident that stalks the marsh edges for fiddler crabs and other mud-dwelling prey.

Up ahead you'll see numerous ditches in the pools. These holes provide deeper water where fish and tiny invertebrates can thrive since they are important in the diets of wading birds and young waterfowl. Shortly you'll come to large, muddy areas that have been created by the thousands of snow geese, who gobble up both the roots and the tips of marsh grasses, leaving this muddy "eatout" behind.

6.0 STOP to examine the refuge upland area.

Fields are maintained here to increase habitat diversity for wildlife. A variety of animal species feed in either the woodland or field edge, using the other habitat for cover and nesting. Watch for deer, rabbits, and songbirds along the road, as well as for Canada geese grazing in the fields.

Check out the trees atop the bluff to your right, where bald and golden eagles have often been spotted during winter months. Other birds of prey, such as ospreys and marsh hawks, are sometimes seen over the ponds.

Continue along, going slightly uphill for about 1 mile. Those open roads cut through the upland area are fire lanes.

7.6 Ride STRAIGHT through the exit gate and turn LEFT.

8.0 ARRIVE at the parking area.

Before leaving, you might enjoy taking the 0.25-mile self-guiding James F. Akers Woodland foot trail through the refuge forest to spot a few of the approximately 200 bird species that have been recorded here. These include the mourning dove, yellow-shafted flicker, downy woodpecker, flycatcher, catbird, and American goldfinch. Juniper, holly, and scrub pine dominate this area, and frequently bobwhites and ring-necked pheasants can be seen along the edge of the woods.

28
Bridgeton

Location: *Cumberland County*
Starting point: *Kmart Shopping Center, Delsea Drive, Vineland*
Terrain: *Flat*
Traffic: *Light*
Round-trip distance pedaled: *66.0 miles*
Highlights: *Wheaton Village, Bridgeton Historic District, Parvin State Park*

South Jersey, famous as a glassmaking center since colonial times, continues to thrive today. Wheaton Village, a stop along this route, commemorates the rich history of glassmaking through demonstrations by skilled craftsmen and the exquisite Museum of American Glass.

This section of the state is also known for its truck farming, and you'll see acres of fruits and vegetables along the route, which justify New Jersey's nickname, the Garden State. Row after row of tomatoes, potatoes, zucchini, corn, and cabbage stretch out into the distance, creating wondrous patterns as you cycle by.

During the first day of this 2-day trip, you'll sample bucolic farm scenery, take a refreshing swim at Parvin Lake (depending on the season), and spend an afternoon exploring historic Bridgeton, which lies along the Cohansey River. On the second day you'll travel south along deserted roads in a semicircle through farmland and marshland to Wheaton Village in Millville.

Park at the Kmart Shopping Center on the west side of Route 47 (Delsea Drive) in Vineland, near the border with Millville. Although personnel at the center report that no permission is necessary to park overnight and no break-ins have been reported, they do caution that you park at your own risk! Cumberland Mall is opposite the highway. Reset your odometer at the exit where it intersects Route 47.

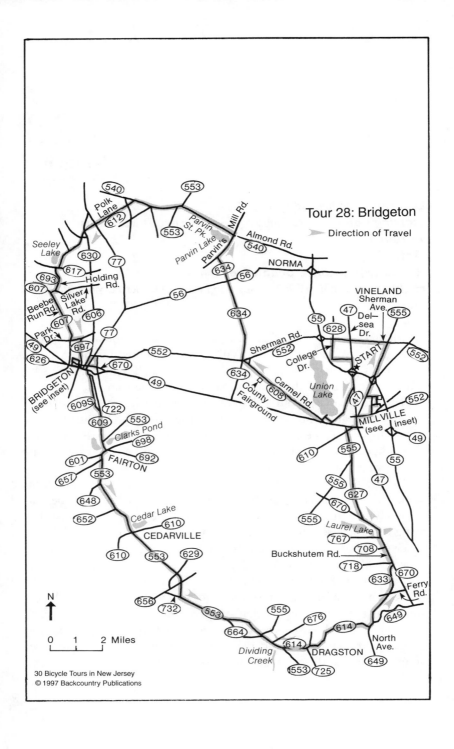

Tour 28: Bridgeton

Direction of Travel

540
553
Polk Lane
612
Parvin St. Pk.
553
Parvin Lake
Parvin's
Mill Rd.
Almond Rd.
540
NORMA

Seeley Lake
630
77
634
56
VINELAND
Sherman Ave.
47
555
693
617
Holding Rd.
Del-sea Dr.
607
Beebe Run Rd.
Silver Lake Rd.
56
634
55
628
607
606
Sherman Rd.
552
College Dr.
START
Park Dr.
77
552
552
49
552
626
697
670
49
722
Union Lake
47
BRIDGETON (see inset)
609S
49
634
Carmel Rd.
608
County Fairground
47
552
MILLVILLE (see inset)
609
722
49
609
553
Clarks Pond
698
610
555
601
FAIRTON
692
555
555
657
553
627
648
670
652
Cedar Lake
610
555
Laurel Lake
CEDARVILLE
767
708
610
553
629
Buckshutem Rd.
718
633
670
656
732
553
Ferry Rd.
664
555
676
614
649
N
614
DRAGSTON
North Ave.
Dividing Creek
553
725
649

0   1   2 Miles

30 Bicycle Tours in New Jersey
© 1997 Backcountry Publications

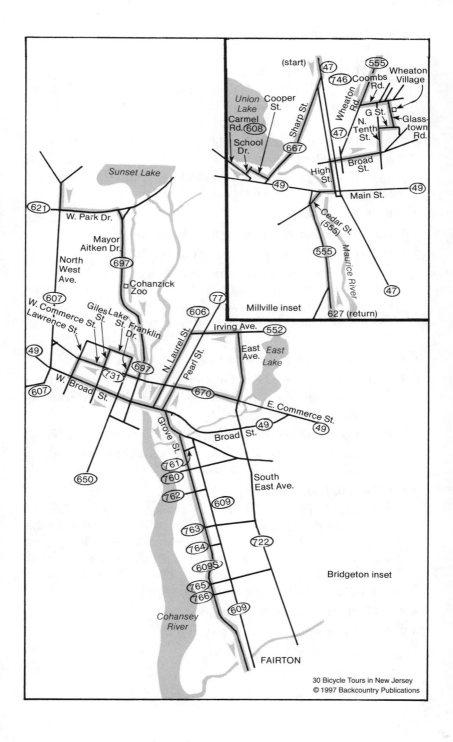

30 Bicycle Tours in New Jersey
© 1997 Backcountry Publications

0.0 RIGHT (south) onto Route 47.

Almost immediately, you'll arrive at the intersection with Route 55, a major artery that leads nowhere, according to natives. There's a lot of traffic, so watch for merging cars in this section.

0.7 Bear RIGHT at the sign for Millville Airport and then RIGHT again onto Sharp Street.

You'll pass a food market at 1.9 miles in Millville before crossing a couple of bridges. Union Lake flanks your right.

2.5 RIGHT onto Cooper Street.

2.8 LEFT at the end of the street onto School Drive.

2.9 RIGHT at the T onto (unmarked) Carmel Road.

You'll ride through a forested area on the right for about 0.5 mile before entering farm country. Traffic is light here—fortunately, because there isn't any shoulder. If you're here on the right day, you might enjoy festivities held year-round at the County Fairground at 6.0 miles.

6.7 LEFT at the T onto Sherman Road.

6.8 RIGHT onto Route 634 at the 4-H sign.

Farms line both sides of this shoulderless road. There is an attractive modern church at 10.5 miles.

11.2 RIGHT onto Parvin's Mill Road at the sign for Parvin State Park.

The park entrance is in less than 1 mile. Rental boats are available at the lake; it's a lovely spot to stop.

12.4 LEFT onto Route 540.

This road, the first one after the park entrance, is unmarked, as are many of the intersections in this area. Route 540 follows along the edge of the park, and you'll have views of the lake for a short while. There's a swimming beach at 12.7 miles where you might want to stop for a dip. As you cycle farther, you'll pass dense woods, farms, and numerous roadside farm stands.

14.8 LEFT at the T as Route 553 joins in.

14.9 RIGHT, continuing on Route 540.

Truck farms abound in this area.

16.6 LEFT onto Route 612, Polk Lane.

This smooth, lightly traveled road leads past more farmland. Depending on the season, there will be huge crops of corn, squash, tomatoes, and potatoes.

20.9 RIGHT at the T onto Route 617.

Serene Seeley Lake is on the right.

21.0 LEFT onto (unmarked) Holding Road.

A slight hill comes as a surprise, adding a bit of variety to an otherwise flat landscape. Pickers can often be seen working these farms.

22.1 RIGHT at the T onto (unmarked) Silver Lake Road.

22.3 LEFT at the T onto (unmarked) Beebe Run Road.

You'll be passing pleasant scenery along this smooth road.

24.4 LEFT onto West Park Drive into the Bridgeton City Park.

24.8 First RIGHT onto (unmarked) Mayor Aitken Drive (Route 697).

The Cohanzick Zoo, on the left at 25.1 miles, is worth a stop. Sip from the unusual "lion" water fountain, refill your canteen, and enjoy the small but interesting collection of animals grouped according to their geographic ranges.

The Nail Museum, former office of the Cumberland Nail and Iron Works, is about 1 mile down the road. In its heyday around 1815, the company employed several hundred people for the production of wrought-iron nails, until these were displaced in the 1890s by the less expensive wire nail.

Glance left as you approach West Commerce Street; this complex of buildings, known locally as the Seven Sisters, contains some of the oldest commercial structures in New Jersey.

25.9 RIGHT onto West Commerce Street.

Bridgeton, reputed to be New Jersey's largest historic district, has more than 2000 houses and buildings on the National Register of Historic Places. Many of the Colonial, Federal, and Victorian houses are still in use today.

As you turn into Commerce Street, note the bright yellow Federal building at 31 West Commerce; built by David Sheppard in 1791 as his private residence, it is the oldest mansion in town.

26.0 RIGHT onto Franklin Drive.

26.1 LEFT onto Lake Street.

Rather than chop down this giant oak, it was left standing in the street. Pedal around it and stop at 25 Lake Street. Built in Gothic Revival style in 1872, this house, known as the House of Seven Gables, served in the past as a private school and as a maternity hospital; it is now an apartment residence.

26.2 LEFT onto Giles Street.

26.3 RIGHT at the stop sign onto West Commerce Street.

The eclectic Victorian house on the right at 137 West Commerce Street, now a funeral home, was built in the 1870s. Its roof is Second Empire, the windows Italianate, the doorway is Colonial Revival, and the porch is Greek Revival.

26.5 LEFT onto Lawrence Street.

Lock your bike onto the iron gate in front of the First Presbyterian Church on the right just beyond the intersection with Broad Street, and take a few minutes to wander among the interesting ancient tombstones in its adjacent cemetery.

26.6 LEFT onto West Broad Street.

At the courthouse on the right, you'll find the bell that rang out to summon people for a formal reading of the Declaration of Independence on July 7, 1776, and to witness the burning of the emblem of British rule. Across the street stands Potter's Tavern, built in 1767, with architecture typical of frame houses built in New Jersey during the 17th and 18th centuries. The tavern served as a meeting place where people talked of liberty and separation from British rule and where the first issue of the *Plain Dealer* was posted. This paper, New Jersey's first, ran for several issues.

27.2 LEFT onto Pearl Street.

27.3 RIGHT onto East Commerce Street.

More than 20,000 arrow points, spears, pots, and shards from the Lenni-Lenape tribe that once lived in the area can be examined at the Woodruff Museum, housed in the basement of the library on the right at 27.4 miles. Hours vary, but the librarian will usually open it upon request; free.

27.7 LEFT onto (unmarked) East Avenue.

If you see East Lake on your left, you've gone too far. There are several historic houses here, including the one at 69 East Avenue, built in 1833 by the mayor of Bridgeton.

28.1 LEFT onto Irving Avenue.

28.4 LEFT onto (unmarked) North Laurel Street.

With so much to see in Bridgeton, it's a good place to explore by foot. Have dinner, find a place to stay, get a good night's sleep, and start out early the next morning.

28.8 LEFT onto East Broad Street.

28.9 RIGHT onto Grove Street at the sign for Fairton, just past the sheriff's office.

30.6 Bear RIGHT onto Route 609.

The Cohanzick Country Club's golf course is on the right in about 0.5 mile; it's open to the public.

31.8 Bear RIGHT onto Route 553.

You'll cross Clarks Pond, a scenic spot.

32.2 RIGHT at the T onto Route 692, then LEFT onto Route 553 South.

This rough road has light traffic and passes farms and produce stands. Cedar Lake (in the town of Cedarville) appears at 35.9 miles on the left and has an inviting swimming beach. Food and drinks are available in town.

At 39.6 miles, follow the main road to the left as Route 732 veers to the right. A swampy pond becomes visible on the right in a couple of miles, and you'll cross a bridge over Dividing Creek at 43.7 miles.

43.9 LEFT after the bridge onto Route 614 to Dragston.

In 1.1 miles, follow the road by turning left and then right immediately after.

47.8 LEFT at the T onto North Avenue (Route 649).

48.0 STRAIGHT ahead as Route 649 veers off to the right.

Continue straight at 49.4 miles as Ferry Road leads to the right. You'll be entering a forested area.

50.8 LEFT at the T onto (unmarked) Buckshutem Road (Route 670).

The headquarters for the Edward G. Bevan Fish and Wildlife Management Area is to your right as you turn. Opportunities for purchasing food or drink are just ahead. At 52.2 miles cross Laurel Lake, a peaceful spot for a break.

52.9 RIGHT onto (unmarked) Route 627 at the sign for Millville.

55.5 STRAIGHT ahead onto what is now Route 555 North.

This road takes you into Millville.

56.6 RIGHT onto Cedar Street (Route 555).

56.8 RIGHT at the T onto Main Street.

Before crossing the Maurice River, you'll come to a convenience store. Riverfront Park is another pleasant place to relax.

57.1 LEFT onto High Street.

Shops of all kinds line Millville's primary thoroughfare.

57.5 RIGHT onto Broad Street.

58.2 LEFT onto North 10th Street.

A small store here has snacks and ice cream.

58.5 RIGHT onto G Street.

58.7 LEFT onto Glasstown Road.

Turn right into the circular driveway in front of the entrance to Wheaton Village at 59.0 miles, and chain your bike to the fence.

The minute you enter Wheaton Village, you'll leave the 20th century behind, for the buildings, streets, and shops within are a re-creation of the styles prevalent in the late 1800s. Inside the impressive Museum of American Glass is a collection of more than 7000 objects ranging from paperweights to fiber optics, Mason jars, and Tiffany masterpieces. Here you'll learn how glass is made and the history of Wheaton Village, which dates back to 1888.

In the Glass Factory, you'll feel the heat from the 2100-degree Fahrenheit furnace as you watch artisans scoop up blobs of molten glass on long rods and shape the oozing, fiery balls into

Take time out to blow your own paperweight at the Museum of Glass
at Wheaton Village.

magnificent colored shapes. As you watch this fascinating process,
you'll hear how it's done, as well. For a reasonable fee, you can
make your own colored paperweight under the supervision of a
glassmaker.

Train buffs can take a short ride aboard the half-scale replica
of an 1863 C.P. Huntington train. Or if you're into crafts, you can

watch tinsmith demonstrations, a potter making traditional hand-thrown and -decorated salt-glazed wares, and woodworking and lampmaking projects.

Before leaving, visit the print shop, have an ice cream at the Victorian-era pharmacy counter, and see the collection of nostalgic items at the General Store. (Open year-round. Hours vary, but normally 10–5 daily from April through December; from January through March, closed Monday and Tuesday; and closed New Year's, Easter, Thanksgiving, and Christmas; fee. Call 609-825-6800 for information on special events.) Lunch and snacks are served at the adjacent restaurant and pub. The Country Inn, adjacent to the village (reservations: 1-800-456-4000) is a great place to stay over for another night if you want to linger. Rates are very reasonable, rooms are attractive and comfortable, and free cookies, coffee, and tea are available in the lobby.

When you've finished exploring the village, continue around the driveway to the right.

59.2 RIGHT onto Glasstown Road.

59.3 LEFT at the T onto Coombs Road.

59.7 RIGHT at the T onto Route 555, Wheaton Road.

Be careful on this wide street as you cross the ramps leading to and from Route 55.

62.1 LEFT onto Sherman Avenue (Route 552).

Cycling is easy along this wide road.

64.5 LEFT onto Route 628.

Cumberland County College, on the right at about 64.8 miles, is in a lovely setting surrounded by pine trees.

65.6 RIGHT onto Route 47.

There are lots of stores along this stretch.

66.0 RIGHT into the Kmart Shopping Center.

29
Belleplain

Location: *Cape May County*
Starting point: *Cedar Square Center, Route 9, Seaville*
Terrain: *Flat*
Traffic: *Light*
Round-trip distance pedaled: *30.0 miles*
Highlights: *Belleplain State Forest, swimming, fishing*

Northern Cape May County is a rural area well endowed with fragrant pine forests and charming byways. Along most of this trip you'll experience complete solitude, especially in the pristine woods found in Belleplain State Forest. Here you can relax and swim in Lake Nummy's cool, clean water or picnic under the shade of fragrant pines.

There is very little traffic on this trip, and because most of the roads have shoulders, you'll be able to spend more time concentrating on the scenery.

Park at the Cedar Square Center on Route 9 in Seaville, just north of the intersection with Route 50. Reset your odometer at the exit from the shopping center where it meets Route 9.

0.0 LEFT (south) onto Route 9.

Traffic can be somewhat heavy here at times, but the road and shoulder are wide. Ice cream, drinks, and groceries are available at 2.7 miles. Magnolia Lake, on the right at 3.0 miles, is a beautiful spot to stop for a moment or two.

3.3 RIGHT onto Main Street (Route 628).

4.6 LEFT at the sign for South Dennis, continuing on Route 628.

7.4 RIGHT onto Route 83.

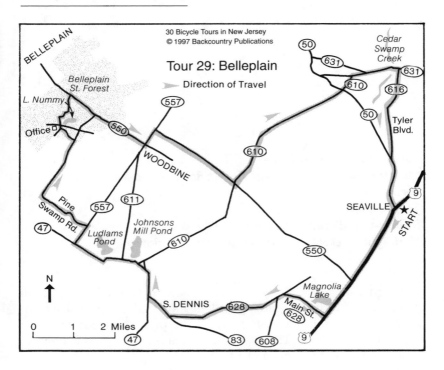

30 Bicycle Tours in New Jersey
© 1997 Backcountry Publications

Tour 29: Belleplain

Direction of Travel

8.1 RIGHT onto Route 47.

Route 47 is a main highway, but it has a wide shoulder most of the way. There is a food market at 8.8 miles, just before two jewel-like ponds come into view on the right.

10.8 RIGHT onto Route 557 (Washington Avenue).

11.3 LEFT onto Pine Swamp Road.

Despite some ruts and potholes, this road is easy to negotiate. You may see an occasional bicyclist in this section thickly wooded with oak and pine. Go slowly: Deer, foxes, cottontails, opossums, squirrels, muskrats, and beavers frequently dart out of the woods onto the roadway.

14.6 LEFT into Belleplain State Forest Recreation Area.

Established in 1928 for public recreation, timber production, wildlife management, and water conservation, Belleplain State

Fishing is one way to relax at Belleplain State Forest..

Forest was named in honor of the last Lenni-Lenape chief to rule in Cape May County. Its stands of pine, oak, and southern white cedar are a feast for the eyes.

Lake Nummy is on the right at 14.9 miles. If the park office is open, it can supply a map of the park and has rest rooms.

15.1 RIGHT onto the park road just past the lake.

You'll arrive at the lakefront beach area in about 0.1 mile. This is a great place for picnicking, swimming, or just taking a nice break amid the trees. When you're ready to continue on, follow the park road and go around the barricade at 15.5 miles. Many branches are strewn along this path. In about 0.5 mile you'll reach a second barricade; go around this one, too.

16.0 RIGHT at the T onto Route 550.

A 7-mile road marker is visible just after you turn. This excellent road skirts along Belleplain State Forest for about 1.5 miles. Route 550 turns LEFT at 18.1 miles as it is joined by Route 557 and then continues RIGHT at 18.5 miles. Soon after, you'll come to Lincoln Park, a local recreation area, and a market.

20.9 LEFT at the stoplight onto Route 610.

Oaks and pines line this wide road. At 24.4 miles you'll pass a church built in 1853 and a large cemetery.

24.4 Bear RIGHT onto Route 631.

This smooth road passes through a swampy area with high grasses and dozens of red-winged blackbirds. Cedar Swamp Creek, formed when underground springs of fresh water broke through the soil in what was previously an ocean floor, is at 26.1 miles. Masses of white cedar eventually took over the rich, moist soil, providing a perfect habitat for wildlife.

26.2 RIGHT onto Route 616 (Tyler Boulevard).

Fortunately this rough, shoulderless road has little traffic.

28.5 LEFT at the T onto Route 50.

An ice cream shop, food market, and several restaurants can be found in this area.

29.9 LEFT onto Route 9.

Arrive at the entrance to Cedar Square Center at 30.0 miles.

30
Cape May

Location: Cape May County
Starting point: Cape May County Park, Route 9, Cape May Court House
Terrain: Flat
Traffic: Moderate
Round-trip distance pedaled: 40.3 miles
Highlights: Victorian houses, beaches, swimming, lighthouse, Cold Spring Village, Wetlands Institute, Cape May "diamonds"

Cape May, one of the oldest seaside resorts on the Atlantic Coast, once attracted such notables as Abraham Lincoln, Franklin Pierce, James Buchanan, and Ulysses S. Grant. In 1903 Henry Ford entered his car in beach races here, trying (unsuccessfully) to lure people into buying stock in his new company. The area is also recognized as an outstanding bird-watching spot, where more than 400 species of birds—including peregrine falcons, bald eagles, and ospreys—can be seen during their spring and fall migrations.

Although this trip is only 40.3 miles long, it includes quite a few places of interest. If you want to linger at some, spend time swimming, or hunt for Cape May "diamonds," consider taking 2 days. (Write to the Cape May Chamber of Commerce, Box 74, Cape May Court House, NJ 08210, for a list of hotels, bed & breakfast inns, and campgrounds.)

Park and begin at Cape May County Park, located on Route 9 about a mile north of Cape May Court House. The park offers picnicking facilities and a small zoo with 100 animals. Special events and concerts are sponsored here during the summer.

Park your car, pedal to the park entrance on Route 9, and reset your odometer.

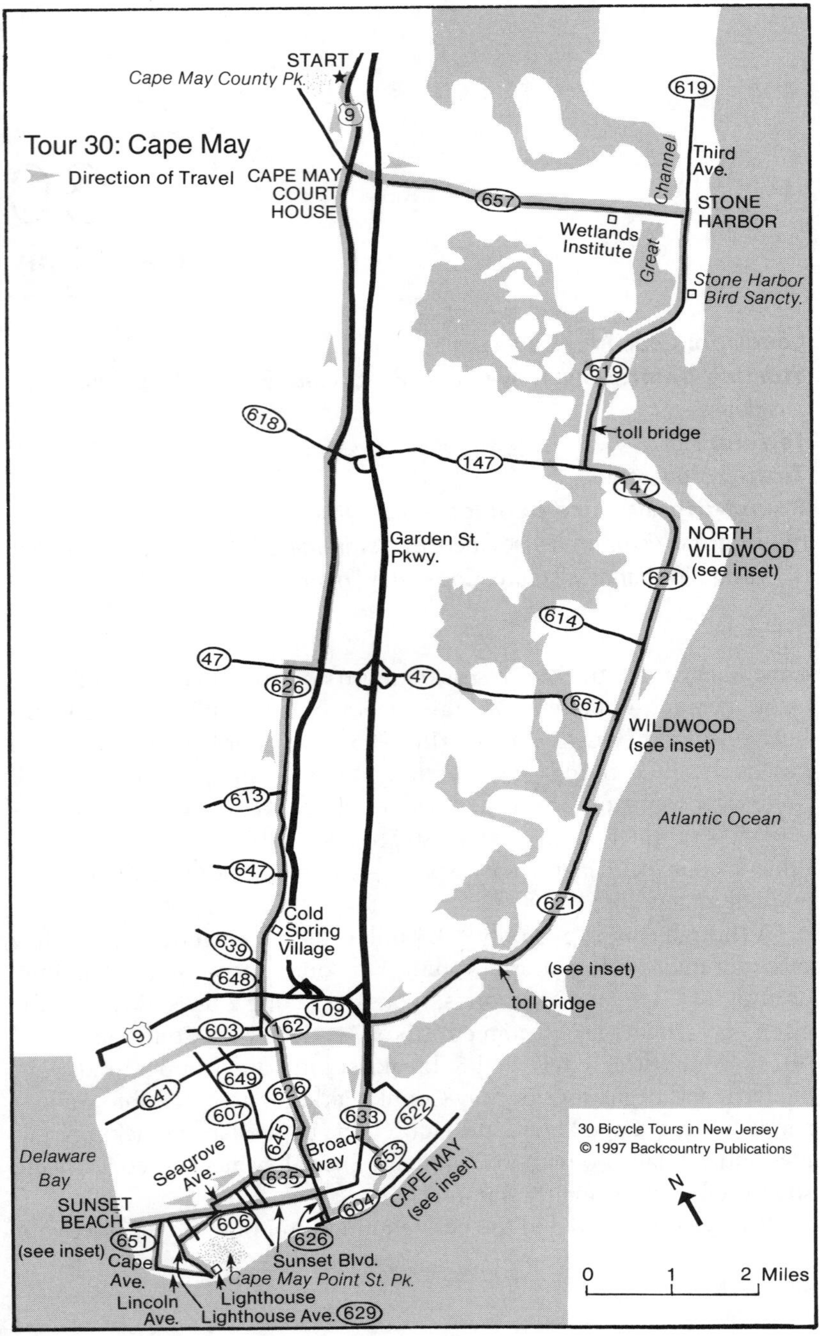

Tour 30: Cape May
Direction of Travel
START
Cape May County Pk.
9
CAPE MAY COURT HOUSE
657
619
Third Ave.
Great Channel
STONE HARBOR
Wetlands Institute
Stone Harbor Bird Sancty.
619
toll bridge
618
147
147
Garden St. Pkwy.
NORTH WILDWOOD (see inset)
621
614
47
47
626
661
WILDWOOD (see inset)
613
Atlantic Ocean
647
621
Cold Spring Village
639
(see inset)
648
toll bridge
109
9
603
162
641
649
626
607
645
633
622
Broadway
653
Delaware Bay
Seagrove Ave.
635
CAPE MAY (see inset)
604
SUNSET BEACH
606
651
626
(see inset)
Cape Ave.
Sunset Blvd.
Cape May Point St. Pk.
Lincoln Ave.
Lighthouse
Lighthouse Ave.
629
30 Bicycle Tours in New Jersey
© 1997 Backcountry Publications
N
0 1 2 Miles

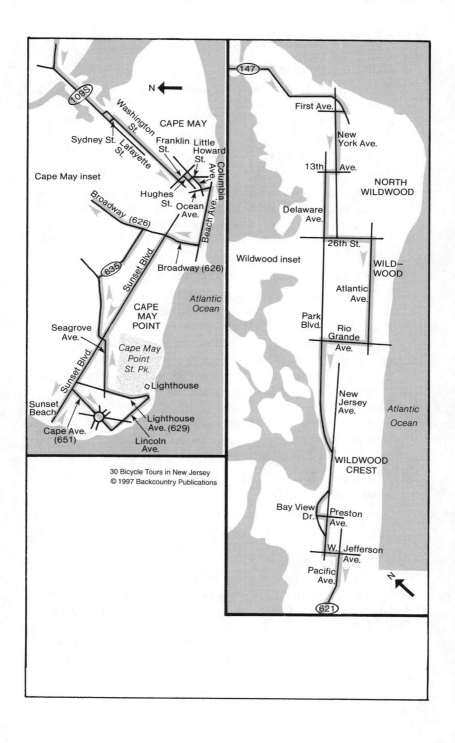

N

CAPE MAY

Washington St.
Sydney St.
Lafayette St.
Franklin St.
Little Howard St.
Columbia Ave.
Beach Ave.

Cape May inset

109S

Hughes St.
Ocean Ave.

Broadway (626)

Broadway (626)

635

Sunset Blvd.

CAPE MAY POINT

Atlantic Ocean

Seagrove Ave.

Cape May Point St. Pk.

Sunset Blvd.

Lighthouse

Sunset Beach

Lighthouse Ave. (629)

Cape Ave. (651)

Lincoln Ave.

147

First Ave.

New York Ave.

13th Ave.

NORTH WILDWOOD

Delaware Ave.

26th St.

Wildwood inset

WILD–WOOD

Atlantic Ave.

Park Blvd.

Rio Grande Ave.

New Jersey Ave.

Atlantic Ocean

WILDWOOD CREST

Bay View Dr.
Preston Ave.

W. Jefferson Ave.

Pacific Ave.

N

621

30 Bicycle Tours in New Jersey
© 1997 Backcountry Publications

0.0 RIGHT (south) onto Route 9.

The Cape May County Museum, located 0.2 mile on the left, contains Native American relics, old tools, household utensils, and artifacts relating to Cape May's early history. (Open September through December and March through June; fee.)

1.1 LEFT onto Route 657.

After crossing the Garden State Parkway, you'll be riding on a wide shoulder alongside heavy traffic, especially during the summer tourist season. The road is lined with tall grasses and marshland. After crossing the wooden bridge at 2.3 miles, look for the Wetlands Institute, which is housed in a lighthouse-shaped building on the right.

3.0 RIGHT into the institute's parking lot.

A film about the surrounding salt marshes and an explanation of their ecological importance is presented at regular intervals. There is also a self-guiding Salt Marsh Trail showing the effects the harsh marsh environment has on plants and animals. Climb the spiral stairs to the observation tower for a bird's-eye view of the 6000-acre marshland and surrounding communities. A rest room and water fountain are in the building. (Open May 15 through October 15 daily, and Tuesday through Saturday from October 15 through May 15; fee. Call 609-368-1211 for hours.)

When you're ready to resume the tour, continue east on Route 657, crossing the bridge into Stone Harbor. Food is available here.

3.8 RIGHT onto Route 619 (Third Avenue) at the sign for Wildwood and Cape May.

Great Channel, part of the Inland Waterway, is to the right; the 21-acre Stone Harbor Bird Sanctuary is on the left at 4.6 miles. Visitors are not admitted, but with binoculars you can spot birds as they fly overhead.

Continuing straight ahead, you'll cross a bridge at 5.2 miles from which there are excellent views of the surrounding marshland, water, and fishing boats. At the end of the bridge there's room to pull over to the side of the road if you want to watch shorebirds and herons feed in the salt marshes to the right. At 6.8 miles you'll cross another bridge, where even cyclists are forced to pay the toll.

Climb the spiral stairs to the observation tower of the Wetlands Institute for a bird's-eye view of the 6000-acre marshland and surrounding communities.

7.2 LEFT at the T onto Route 147 toward Wildwood.

You'll find lots of restaurants here, and in a short distance you'll cross a rickety wooden bridge. On most days there's a good deal of traffic, but thankfully there's a wide shoulder. Route 147 zigzags as you approach Wildwood. Follow signs for Cape May.

8.7 RIGHT onto First Avenue.

8.8 LEFT onto New York Avenue.

Marinas are on the right.

9.4 RIGHT onto 13th Avenue.

9.5 LEFT onto Delaware Avenue.

Water and rest rooms are available at 9.9 miles within the park.

10.1 LEFT onto 26th Street.

10.6 RIGHT onto Atlantic Avenue.

This main drag has many motels and restaurants. The beach and boardwalk are to the left. (A beach-use fee is charged.)

11.6 RIGHT onto Rio Grande Avenue.

12.0 LEFT onto Park Boulevard.

A selection of fast-food places dots the intersection. Excursion and fishing boats are on the right at 12.7 miles.

13.2 RIGHT onto New Jersey Avenue.

Sailboat rentals are available by the hour here.

13.4 Bear RIGHT onto Bay View Drive.

13.8 LEFT onto Preston Avenue.

13.9 RIGHT onto New Jersey Avenue.

14.3 LEFT onto West Jefferson Avenue.

14.4 RIGHT onto Pacific Avenue (Route 621).

Have change ready for another toll bridge at 15.7 miles. This nautical stretch passes by seafood markets, restaurants, and a yacht basin.

17.4 LEFT at the T at the sign for Cape May onto Route 109 South.

USE CAUTION at this busy intersection.

18.2 LEFT onto Sydney Street.

18.3 RIGHT onto Washington Street.

Cape May, designated a National Historic Landmark, has more than 600 buildings dating from more than 100 years ago. Architecture buffs will appreciate the variety of cupolas. Supposedly the "captain's walk" cupola facing the sea was where a wife watched for her husband's returning ship, and the "widow's walk" was an open area on the roof used as a retreat for the wife who had watched in vain.

Stop at the Emlen Physick House at 1050 Washington Street for a tour of this 16-room mansion, designed in the stick style in 1878. Inside is a collection of Victorian furniture, toys, tools, and costumes. Next door, in the former carriage house, you can examine the latest exhibit on display by the Cape May County Art League, fill your canteen, or use the rest room. (Open daily except Friday; there's an admission fee to the Physick House only.) You'll pass another ornate Victorian house at 720 Washington Street.

19.1 LEFT onto Franklin Street.

19.2 RIGHT onto Hughes Street.

The houses on this street have many interesting features; look for the dormer windows at 655 Hughes Street and the brightly painted gingerbread at 654 Hughes.

19.3 LEFT onto Little Howard Street, then RIGHT onto Columbia Avenue.

Numerous bed & breakfast inns line Columbia Avenue. The impressive house at 635 Columbia Avenue was built in 1856 as a club for southern gentlemen. If you're interested in seeing more of these charming houses, cycle up and down the local streets, because the route will now follow the ocean.

19.4 LEFT onto (unmarked) Ocean Avenue.

19.5 RIGHT onto Beach Avenue.

Hotels and restaurants are jammed during summer months. If you want to take a dip, bike racks are available at each beach entry, but there's a fee for using the beach.

20.2 RIGHT onto Broadway (Route 626).

20.5 LEFT onto Sunset Boulevard (Route 606).

22.7 STOP at the dead end.

You've reached Sunset Beach, the favorite hunting grounds for those who search the sands for quartz pebbles known as Cape May diamonds. That weird, partially submerged hulk in front of you is the *Atlantus,* an experimental concrete ship that was towed here after it foundered in a storm in 1926. It was one of 14 built during World War I.

After filling your bags with "diamonds," turn back onto Route 606.

23.1 RIGHT onto Cape Avenue, Route 651.

Stay on Cape Avenue around the traffic circle.

23.7 LEFT at the end of the street onto Lincoln Avenue.

You'll be riding along the edge of large sand dunes.

24.2 LEFT at the end of the street onto Lighthouse Avenue, Route 629.

Cape May Point Lighthouse, one of the oldest lighthouses still actively commissioned by the Coast Guard as a navigational aid, dates to 1859 and stands 165 feet above ground level. Its light, visible for 19 miles, goes on automatically at dusk.

24.3 RIGHT into Cape May Point State Park.

This is a great place to sit and listen to the pounding surf. The park offers picnicking, rest rooms, and a 3-mile walking trail through a natural area.

When you're ready to continue on, follow the one-way signs out of the park.

24.6 RIGHT onto Lighthouse Avenue.

25.0 RIGHT onto Seagrove Avenue.

Cross Sunset Boulevard at 25.5 miles.

26.1 STRAIGHT ahead on what is now Route 635.

26.8 LEFT onto Route 626 (Broadway).

Drinks are available along this road. You'll cross Route 9 at 29.0 miles before coming to the Cold Spring Presbyterian Church, built in 1823, and a huge cemetery.

29.7 RIGHT at the entrance to Historic Cold Spring Village.

Representing a typical 19th-century south Jersey farm village, all of these 15 structures were saved from destruction and brought here to create a live outdoor museum consisting of crafts shops, a country store, and a restaurant. (Open daily 10–sunset, Memorial Day to the end of September; fee.)

29.8 RIGHT (north) onto Route 626.

A food market is at 31.8 miles.

33.0 RIGHT onto Route 47.

33.3 LEFT (north) onto Route 9.

Eating places abound at this intersection. Although Route 9 is a major artery farther north, it's just a country road here. You'll pass the two-story wooden 1850 courthouse, for which the community of Cape May Court House is named, at 38.8 miles.

40.3 ARRIVE at the entrance to Cape May County Park.

Appendix

Overnight Accommodations

Motels

Many hotels, motels, inns, and bed & breakfast accommodations offer special weekend package deals. Listed below are toll-free reservation numbers for chains located within the state.

Best Western International, Inc., 1-800-528-1234

Comfort Inns, 1-800-228-5150

Country Inn Hotel, 1-800-456-4000

Courtyards by Marriott, 1-800-321-2211

Days Inns, 1-800-325-2525

Doubletree, Inc., 1-800-528-0444

Econo Lodges of America, 1-800-446-6900

Embassy Suites, 1-800-362-2779

Friendship Inns of America International, 1-800-453-4511

Hampton Inns, 1-800-426-7866

Hilton Hotels Corp., 1-800-445-8667

Holiday Inns, Inc., 1-800-465-4329

Howard Johnson, 1-800-654-2000

Hyatt Corp., 1-800-228-9000

Loews Hotels, 1-800-223-0888

Mariott Hotels, 1-800-228-9290

Quality Inns, 1-800-228-5151

Radisson Hotel Corp., 1-800-333-3333

Ramada Inns, 1-800-272-6232

Red Carpet/Scottish Inns, 1-800-251-1962

Red Roof Inns, 1-800-843-7663

Residence Inns by Marriott, 1-800-331-3131

Sheraton Hotels and Inns, 1-800-325-3535

Super 8 Motels, 1-800-843-1991

Travelodge International Inc./Viscount, 1-800-255-3050

Trusthouse Forte Hotels, 1-800-225-5843

Budget motel accommodations are listed in the *National Directory of Budget Motels* (New York: Pilot Books).

Bed & Breakfasts
For bed & breakfast accommodations, consult *Bed & Breakfast U.S.A.* (New York: Dutton), and *Bed & Breakfast in the Mid-Atlantic States* (Chester, CT: Globe Pequot), or try one of the following accommodations recommended by the Bed & Breakfast Innkeepers Association of New Jersey, PO Box 108, Spring Lake, NJ 07762.

Skylands Region
Crossed Keys, 289 Pequest Road, Andover, 973-786-6661

Parrot Mill Inn, 47 Main Street, Chatham, 973-635-7722

Amber House, 66 Leigh Street, Clinton, 908-735-7881

Cabbage Rose Inn, 162 Main Street, Flemington, 908-788-0247

Jerica Hill Inn, 96 Broad Street, Flemington, 908-782-8234

Hunterdon House, 12 Bridge Street, Frenchtown, 908-996-3632

Apple Valley Inn, 517 & Route 565, Glenwood, 973-764-3735

Bridge Street House, 75 Bridge Street, Lambertville, 609-397-2503

Chimney Hill Farm, 207 Goat Hill Road, Lambertville, 609-397-1516

Chestnut Hill on the Delaware, 63 Church, Milford, 908-995-9761

The Wooden Duck, 140 Goodale Road, Newton, 973-300-0395

Whistling Swan Inn, 110 Main Street, Stanhope, 973-347-6369

Stewart Inn, 706 South Main Street, Stewartsville, 908-479-6060

The Woolverton Inn, 6 Woolverton Road, Stockton, 609-397-0802

Holly Thorn, 143 Readington Road, Whitehouse, 908-534-1616

Shore Region

Atlantic View Inn, 20 Woodland Avenue, Avon-by-the-Sea, 732-774-8505

The Sands B&B Inn, 42 Sylvania Avenue, Avon-by-the-Sea, 732-776-8386

The Summer House, 101 Sylvania Avenue, Avon-by-the-Sea, 732-775-3992

Bay Head Gables, 200 Main Street, Bay Head, 732-892-9844

Bay Head Harbor Inn, 676 Main Avenue, Bay Head, 732-899-0767

Conovers Bay Head Inn, 646 Main Avenue, Bay Head, 732-892-4664

Amber Street Inn, 118 Amber Street, Beach Haven, 609-492-1611

Victoria Guest House, 126 Amber Street, Beach Haven, 609-492-4154

House By The Sea, 406 Fifth Avenue, Belmar, 732-681-8386

The Inn at the Shore, 301 Fourth Avenue, Belmar, 732-681-3762

The Seaflower, 110 Ninth Avenue, Belmar, 732-681-6006

SeaScape Manor, 3 Grand Tour, Highlands, 732-291-8467

Goose N. Berry Inn, 190 North Main Street, Manahawkin, 609-597-6350

Carol Inn, 11 Pitman Avenue, Ocean Grove, 732-502-0303

Pine Tree Inn, 10 Main Avenue, Ocean Grove, 732-775-3264

Cashelmara Inn, 22 Lakeside Avenue, Oceanside, 732-776-8727

Beacon House, 104 Beacon Boulevard, Sea Girt, 732-449-5835

Ashling Cottage, 106 Sussex Avenue, Spring Lake, 732-449-3553

Carriage House, 208 Jersey Avenue, Spring Lake, 732-449-1332

Hamilton House Inn, 15 Mercer Avenue, Spring Lake, 732-449-8282

Hollycroft Inn, PO Box 448, Spring Lake, 732-681-2254

Johnson House Inn, 25 Tuttle Avenue, Spring Lake, 732-449-1860

La Maison, 404 Jersey Avenue, Spring Lake, 1-800-276-2088

Mountain House, 120 Ludlow Avenue, Spring Lake, 732-449-5177

Normandy Inn, 21 Tuttle Avenue, Spring Lake, 732-449-7172

Sea Crest by the Sea, 19 Tuttle Avenue, Spring Lake, 732-449-9031

Spring Lake Inn, 104 Salem Avenue, Spring Lake, 732-449-2010

Victoria House, 214 Monmouth Avenue, Spring Lake, 732-974-1882

White Lilac Inn, 414 Central Avenue, Spring Lake, 732-449-0211

Greater Atlantic City

Abbott House, 6056 Main Street, Mays Landing, 609-625-4400

Carisbrooke Inn, 105 South Little Rock Avenue, Ventnor, 609-822-6392

Southern Shore

The Abbey, Columbia Avenue, Cape May, 609-884-4506

Brass Bed, 719 Columbia Avenue, Cape May, 609-884-2302

Cape Mey's Inn, 202 Ocean Street, Cape May, 609-884-7793

Cliveden Inn, 709 Columbia Avenue, Cape May, 609-884-4516

Columns by the Sea, 1513 Beach Drive, Cape May, 609-884-2228

Duke of Windsor, 817 Washington Street, Cape May, 609-884-1355

Fairthorne B&B, 111 Ocean Street, Cape May, 609-884-8791

Henry Sawyer Inn, 722 Columbia Avenue, Cape May, 609-884-5667

Inn at 22 Jackson, 22 Jackson Street, Cape May, 609-884-2226

Inn on Ocean, 25 Ocean Street, Cape May, 1-800-304-4477

John F. Craig House, 609 Columbia Avenue, Cape May, 609-884-0100

Kelly's Celtic Inn, 24 Ocean Street, Cape May, 609-898-1999

King's Cottage, 9 Perry Street, Cape May, 609-884-0415

Leith Hall, 22 Ocean Street, Cape May, 609-884-1934

Mainstay Inn, 635 Columbia Avenue, Cape May, 609-884-8690

Manor House, 612 Hughes Street, Cape May, 609-884-4710

Mason Cottage, 625 Columbia Avenue, Cape May, 609-884-3358

Moffitt House, 715 Broadway, Cape May, 609-898-0915

Perry Street Inn, 29 Perry Street, Cape May, 1-800-297-3779

The Queen Victoria, 102 Ocean Street, Cape May, 609-884-8702

The Stetson Inn, 725 Kearney Avenue, Cape May, 609-884-1724

The Summer Cottage Inn, 613 Columbia Avenue, Cape May, 609-884-4948

Twin Gables, 731 Columbia Avenue, Cape May, 609-884-7332

White Dove Cottage, 619 Hughes Street, Cape May, 1-800-321-3683

Woodleigh House, 808 Washington Street, Cape May, 609-884-7123

Henry Ludlam Inn, 1336 Route 47, Dennisville, 609-861-5847

Candlelight Inn, 2310 Central Avenue, North Wildwood, 609-522-6200

State Campgrounds

Allaire State Park, Route 524, Farmingdale 07727; 732-938-2371

Allamuchy Mountain State Park, Stephen's Section, Hackettstown 07840; 908-852-3790

Bass River State Forest, Stage Road, New Gretna 08824; 609-296-1114

Belleplain State Forest, Meisle Road, Woodbine 08270; 609-861-2404

Bull's Island Section, Delaware & Raritan Canal Park, 2185 Daniel Bray Highway, Stockton 08559; 609-397-2949

Cheesequake State Park, Matawan 07747; 732-566-2161

High Point State Park, 1480 State Route 23, Sussex 07461; 973-875-4800

Jenny Jump State Forest, Shiloh Road, Hope 07844; 908-459-4366

Lebanon State Forest, Route 72, New Lisbon 08064; 609-726-1191

Parvin State Park, Parvin Mill Road, Elmer 08318; 856-358-8616

Round Valley Recreation Area, Lebanon-Stanton Road, Lebanon 08833; 908-236-6355

Spruce Run State Park, 289 Van Syckels Road, Clinton 08809; 908-638-8572

Stokes State Forest, 1 Coursen Road, Branchville 07826; 201-948-3820

Swartswood State Park, East Shore Drive, Swartswood 07877; 973-383-5230

Voorhees State Park, Route 513, Glen Gardner 08826; 908-638-6969

Wawayanda State Park, Box 198, Highland Lakes 07422; 973-853-4462

Wharton State Forest, Batsto, RD 9, Hammonton 08037; 609-268-0444

Worthington State Forest, Old Mine Road, Columbia 07832; 908-841-9575

For a listing of private campgrounds, consult the *Trailer Life Campground/RV Park & Services Directory* (Ventura, CA: TL Enterprises) and the *KOA Campgrounds Directory* (Billings, MT: Kampgrounds of America).

Bicycle Shops

Absecon: Bud's Bikes, 125 New Jersey Avenue, 609-641-8060

Allendale: Richlyn Bike Shop, 317 Franklin Turnpike, 201-825-0952

Andover: Cycle Center of Andover, Route 206, 973-786-6350

Asbury Park: Allenhurst Cycle Shop, 316 Main Street, 908-517-0777

Atlantic City: Bike World, North Michigan Avenue, 609-345-0077

Atlantic Highlands: Atlantic Cyclery, 188 First Avenue, 732-291-2664; Mike's Bikes, 46 First Avenue, 732-291-8822

Avalon: Hollywood Bicycle Center, 2544 Dune Drive, 609-967-5846

Barnegat: Roy's Barnegat Bicycle Ranch, 107 South Main Street, 609-698-6627

Bayonne: Eddy's Cycle City, 635 Broadway, 201-339-3722; RG's Bicycle Shop, 890 Broadway, 201-823-0872

Beach Haven: Brigg's Bicycles, 8401 Long Beach Boulevard, 609-492-1143

Beachwood: Eckert's Bicycles, 101 State Highway 166, 732-349-2333

Bedminster: Alan's Bicycle Shop, 355 Route 202 South, 908-234-2821

Belle Meade: Wheel Life Cycle & Fitness, 1109 Route 206 South, 908-874-0949

Belmar: DJ's Cycles, 1318 15th Street, 732-681-8228; Glendola Bicycle, 2709 Belmar Boulevard, 732-681-5264

Belvidere: Wheelmasters' Bicycle Shop, 12 Hardwick Street, 908-475-5658

Bergenfield: Bicycle Shop, 24 North Washington Avenue, 201-384-2525

Berlin: American Bicycle Tours, Inc., 92 State Highway 73, 856-753-8687

Blackwood: Bike Line of Turnersville, Cross Keys Commons, 856-875-1910

Bloomfield: Brookdale Cycle, 1292 Broad Street, 973-338-8908; Bloomfield Bike, Inc., 545 Bloomfield Avenue, 973-429-9213

Bogota: Cosmic Wheel, 78 West Main Street, 201-487-3733

Bridgeton: Green Acres Bike Shop, Bridgeton-Millville Pike, 609-455-7531

Bridgewater: Spoke-N-Wheel, 564 State Route 28, 732-271-2555

Brielle: Brielle Cyclery, 205 Union Avenue, 732-528-9121

Caldwell: Bike Land, 461 Bloomfield Avenue, 973-403-3330

Cape May: Hale Sports Cycling, 5 Mechanic Street, 609-465-3126; Steck's Bike Rental, 319 Beach Drive, 609-884-1188; Village Bicycle Shop, 2 Victorian Village Plaza, 609-884-8500

Chatham: Bike Corner, Inc., 453 Main Street, 973-635-1920; Bike Land, 219 Main Street, 973-635-8066

Cheesequake: Bicycle World, 155B State Highway 34, 732-566-7710

Chester: Nelson's Cycle Shop, Highway 24, 908-879-7677

Cherry Hill: Camden County Bicycle Center, 620 Haddonfield Road, 856-663-0855; Erlton Bicycle Shop, 1011 State Highway 70, 856-428-2344

Clarksburg: Bill's Bike Shop, 62 Spring Road, 609-259-7537

Clifton: Clifton Speed Center, 1074 Main Avenue, 973-779-9002

Clinton: Clinton Bicycle Shop, 51 Main Street, 908-735-5451

Closter: All-County Schwinn Cyclery, 237 Closter Dock Road, 201-768-3086

Colonia: Colonia Bike & Repair Shop, 1199 St. Georges Avenue, 732-634-5225

Cranford: Cranford Bike Shop, 103 North Union Avenue, 908-272-0184

Denville: Ultra Sports Bike Shop, 286 US Highway 46, 973-625-2900

Dunellen: Bike Line of Greenbrook, 215 US Highway 22, 732-424-1222

East Brunswick: Route 18 Cycle & Fitness, 1177 Route 18, 732-651-8080

Eatontown: Budget Bicycles, 137 State Highway 35, 732-542-6488

Edison: Bike N Gear, 531 Old Post Road, 732-287-6996

Elizabeth: Aaron's Bicycle Shop, 804 First Avenue, 908-352-7454; New Jersey Cycle, 421 North Broad Street, 908-352-9333

Elmwood Park: Sam's Bicycle & Repairs, 252 Broadway, 201-797-5819

Englewood: Bike Masters, 11 Bennett Road, 201-569-3773

Fair Lawn: Amber Cyclery, 1102 River Road, 201-797-5600; Original Bike Shop, 1106 Saddle River Road, 201-791-6555

Flemington: Pete's Bike Shop, 105 Route 31, 908-782-5935

Fort Lee: Strictly Bicycles, 521 Main Street, 201-944-7074

Freehold: Freehold Bicycles, 85 Village Center Drive, 732-431-0266; Fun Town, US Highway 9, 732-780-5750

Frenchtown: Freeman's Bicycle Shop, 52 Bridge Street, 908-996-7712

Glenwood: Vernon Bicycle, 4 Vernon Crossing, 973-764-7775

Greenbrook: Bike Line, 215B US Highway 22 East, 732-424-1222

Hackensack: Hackensack Bicycles, 205 Main Street, 201-488-4466

Hackettstown: Alpine Ski and Bike, 207 Mountain Avenue, 908-852-0852

Hammonton: Pro Pedals, 684 South White Horse Pike, 908-561-3030

Harrison: Olympic Cycle, 317 Harrison Avenue, 973-481-2666

Hasbrouck Heights: Afco Cycle, 193 Boulevard, 201-288-8841

Hawthorne: Bike Pad, 298 Lafayette Avenue, 973-427-9400; Hogies Cycle Shop, 1160 Goffle Road, 973-427-2323

Hazlet: Michael's Bicycle, 2857 State Route 35, 732-739-0333

Highland Park: Highland Park Cyclery, 137 Raritan Avenue, 732-572-6775

Hightstown: Speedway Bicycle Shop, State Highway 33, 609-443-3320

Howell: Brielle Cyclery, 40 Ramtown-Greenville Road, 732-840-9447; Bicycle World, 2449 US Highway 9, 732-431-5610

Irvington: OK Bike Shop, 1090 Clinton Avenue, 973-371-4473; Village Bicycle Shoppe, 858 Stuyvesant Avenue, 973-374-3316

Jersey City: SDS Bicycle Shop, 351 Palisade Avenue, 201-656-5472

Keyport: Gallery 35 Used Bicycles, State Highway 35, 732-739-0978

Lake Hopatcong: Route 15 Bicycle Outlet, Lake Side Shopping Center, Route 15, 973-663-1935

Lakewood: Bicycles Unlimited, 67 East County Line Road, 732-363-2453; Mone Auto Supply, 244 Main Street, 732-363-1345

Lambertville: Wheelfine Imports, Route 518 and Hunter Road, 609-397-3403

Liberty Corner: Liberty Corner Cycle, Main Street, 908-580-9222

Lincoln Park: Bicycle Tech, 246 Main Street, 973-694-6775

Linden: Andy's Cycle Center, 22 West St. Georges Avenue, 908-486-3032; Bicycle Factory Outlet, 631 East Elizabeth Avenue, 908-486-3700; New Jersey Cycle, 910 West St. Georges Avenue, 908-925-1721

Lyndhurst: Meadowlands Cycle Center, 31 Ridge Road, 201-935-5115

Little Falls: Bike Shop at The Ski Barn, 125 Paterson Avenue, 973-256-8585

Long Branch: DJ's Cycles & Fitness, 94 Brighton Avenue, 732-870-2277; Peddler Bicycles, 150 Ocean Boulevard, 908-229-6623

Madison: Madison Bicycle Shop, 14 Kings Road, 973-377-6616

Manahawkin: Brigg's Bicycles, 63 East Bay Avenue, 609-597-5999

Manasquan: Manasquan Bicycle Service, 128 Main Street, 732-223-2444

Manville: Spoke-N-Wheel, 43 South Main Street, 908-526-9307

Marlboro: Bicycle Hub, 455 County Road 520, 732-972-8822

Marlton: Peddler Bicycle Shop, 70 East Main Street, 856-428-8439

Medford: Bike Line, 185 Route 70, 609-654-6868; Genie Cyclery, Skeet and Dixontown Roads, 908-953-0200

Mercerville: Bernie's Bicycle & Fitness Center, 111 Route 33, 732-586-5126

Middlesex: Cycle Craft, 409 Bound Brook Road, 1-800-771-2453

Millburn: Millburn Bicycle Shop, 20 Main Street, 973-376-0001

Millville: Green Acres Bike Shop, Route 49, 609-455-7531; Millville Tire Service, 225 North High Street, 609-825-5555

Metuchen: Metuchen Bicycle Sales & Service, 457 Main Street, 732-548-1954

Monmouth Junction: Halter's Cycle & Fitness, 4095 US Highway 1, 609-275-5600

Montclair: Diamond Cycle, 409 Bloomfield Avenue, 973-509-0233; Greenbrook Bikery, 127 Valley Road, 973-744-7252

Moorestown: Workman's Bike Center, 79 East Main Street, 856-234-6286

Morristown: Marty's Reliable Cycle, 173 Speedwell Avenue, 201-538-7773

Mount Holly: Chip-N-Dale Bike Shop, 1240 Monmouth Road, 609-261-1981

New Brunswick: Kim's Bike Shop, 85 French Street, 732-846-3880

Newton: Bike Stop, Route 206, Ames Plaza, 973-579-5434

Norma: Tommy's Bicycles, Almond Road, 856-692-9146

North Bergen: James Vincent Bicycles, 8505 Bergenline Avenue, 201-869-1901

North Wildwood: Algie's Place, 114 East 17th Avenue, 609-729-5669

Nutley: Nutley Bike Shop, 307 Franklin Avenue, 973-667-1100

Oakland: Pedal Sports, 20 Elm Street, 201-337-9380

Oaklyn: Matson's Schwinn Cyclery, 629 White Horse Pike, 856-854-1152

Ocean City: Annarellis Bicycle Store, 1014 Asbury Avenue, 609-399-2238; Ocean City Bicycle Center, Eighth Avenue, 609-399-5550; Pat's Bicycles, 613 East Eighth Street, 609-399-5220

Old Bridge: The Original Bike Shop, 191 Englishtown Road, 732-251-3757; Bike Line, 3058 US Highway 9, 732-607-0150

Orange: Orange Bicycle Shop, 216 Main Street, 973-678-2987

Palisades Park: Academy Schwinn, 54 Grand Avenue, 201-943-6505

Paramus: Bike Shop at The Ski Barn, 846 North State Route 17, 201-445-9070; Bicycle Shop, 308 East State Route 4, 201-489-1717; Campmor Bike Shop, 810 Route 17 North, 201-445-5000; Paramus Cycle, 23 North Farview Avenue, 201-368-8242

Park Ridge: Cyclesport, 1 Hawthorne Avenue, Depot Square, 201-391-5269

Parsippany: Cycle Craft, 123 Route 46, 973-227-4462

Paterson: Paterson Bike Shop, 370 Main Street, 973-278-1880

Perth Amboy: Jerry & Stan's Bicycle Shop, 442 Amboy Avenue, 732-442-4370

Plainfield: George's Bicycle Shop, 123 Watchung Avenue, 908-757-0030

Point Pleasant Beach: A1 Bicycles, 642 Arnold Avenue, 732-295-2299; Point Pleasant Bicycle, 2701 Bridge Avenue, 732-899-9755

Pompton Lakes: Pompton Cycle Center, 127 Wanaque Avenue, 973-835-6339

Pompton Plains: Bicycle Source, 679 State Route 23, 973-835-7595

Princeton: Bike Shop at The Ski Barn, 29 Emmons Drive, 609-520-0741; Jay's Cycles, 249 Nassau Street, 609-924-7233; Kopp's Cycle, 38 Spring Street, 609-924-1052

Rahway: Anthony's Bike & Key Shop, 1537 Irving Street, 732-388-1198

Ramsey: Ramsey Bicycle & Ski Shop, 44 East Main Street, 201-327-9480

Ridgefield Park: Park Cycle & Sport Center, 184 Main Street, 201-641-0117

Ridgewood: EuroCycle, 580 North Maple Avenue, 201-251-0990

Rochelle Park: Bike Shop, 108 Route 46, 973-478-6709; The Bikeworks, 383 Rochelle Avenue, 201-843-6409

Rockaway Township: Ultra Sports Bicycle Shop, 285 US Highway 46, 973-625-2900

Saddle Brook: The Original Bike Shop, 108 US Highway 46, 973-478-6555

Scotch Plains: The Bike Stand, 360 Park Avenue, 908-322-9022

Sea Isle City: Hollywood Bicycle Center, 4601 Landis Avenue, 609-263-0232; Vince's Bikes, 4012 Pleasure Avenue, 609-263-3186

Seaside Park: Tyres Bicycles, 1900 Boulevard, 732-830-2050

Sewell: Genie Cyclery, Center Square Shopping, 609-582-0800

Shrewsbury: Shrewsbury Bicycle, Inc., 765 Broad Street, 732-741-2799

Somerdale: Ricco's Cyclery, 600 South White Horse Pike, 856-783-3035

Somerset: Bike N Gear, 1695 Amwell Road, 732-873-0212; Franklin Bicycle Center, 853 Hamilton Street, 732-249-4544

Somers Point: Village Schwinn Shop, 606 New Road, 609-927-3775

Somerville: Gregg's Bike Town, 134-B East Main, 908-725-2060; International Bicycles, 254 US Highway 206, 908-359-2700; Quigley's Bicycle Shop, 605 Westminster Court, 908-725-8794; Turner's Somerville Cyclery, 34 East Main Street, 908-725-5008

South Amboy: Hay's Bicycle Shop, State Highway 35, 732-727-3799

South Brunswick: Halter's Cycles, Route 1, 732-329-9022

South Plainfield: South Plainfield Bike Shop, 224 Hamilton Boulevard, 908-755-6969

South River: Bike N Gear, 89 Main Street, 732-257-1890; Stan's Bicycle Shop, 89 Main Street, 732-257-1890

South Somerville: International Bicycles, 254 US Highway 206, 908-359-2700

South Plainfield: T.C. Cycles, 728 Clinton Avenue, 908-756-1449

Sparta: Bike Stop, 9 Main Street, 973-729-7775

Spotswood: Bicycle Rack, 365 Spotswood/Englishtown Road, 732-251-5255

Stirling: High Gear Cyclery, Inc., 1153 Valley Road, 908-647-2010

Stone Harbor: Harbor Bike and Beach Shop, 9228 3rd Avenue, 609-368-3691

Summit: Cycle Palace, 21 Industrial Place, 908-273-0003

Sussex: Sussex Bike & Sport Shop, 155 Route 23, 973-875-6565

Teaneck: Amber Cyclery, 764 Palisade Avenue, 201-836-0104

Tenafly: Tenafly Bicycle Workshop, Inc., 175 County Road, 201-568-9372

Toms River: Beacon Cycling & Fitness, 575 Fischer Boulevard, 732-929-2999; Padi's Pedal Power, 1177 Fischer Boulevard, 732-270-5920; Jerry's Bicycle Shop, 1522 Route 37, 732-929-1155

Totowa: Bob's Bicycle Emporium, 151 Union Boulevard, 973-942-5972

Trenton: Bernie's Bicycle & Fitness Center, 111 Highway 33, 609-586-5126; Economy Bicycle Shop, 31 George Dye Road, 609-586-0150; Hamilton Bike & Fitness, 1111 Highway 33, 609-584-1908; Knapp's Cyclery, 1833 North Olden Avenue, 609-883-5665

Union: Victory Bicycle, 2559 Morris Avenue, 908-686-2383

Union City: Union Cycle Center, 4531 Bergenline Avenue, 201-863-8737

Ventnor City: AAAA Bike Shop, 5300 Ventnor Avenue, 609-487-0808

Vernon: Bike & Board, 317 Route 94, 973-764-6870

Vineland: Ed's Bike Shop, 1377 North Delsea Drive, 856-691-5757; S & R Schwinn Sales, 3419 South Delsea Drive, 856-327-1311; Jerry's Bicycle Shop, State Highway 37, 732-929-1155

Washington: McCormick's Bicycle Shop, 57 Youmans Avenue, 908-689-0385

Wayne: Amber Cyclery, 1275 State Route 23, 973-694-5252; 4 Sons Cyclery, 1154 Hamburg Turnpike, 973-696-5005; Perlmutter's Bike Shop, 179 Hamburg Turnpike, 973-956-1254; Willowbrook Bicycles & Fitness, 973-812-9119

West Berlin: Al's Bike Repair, 142 Haddon Avenue, 856-767-0751; Bike Line of Berlin, Berlin Circle, 856-753-7433

West Long Branch: Cag's Cycles, 821 Broadway, 732-229-6683; Precision Cycles, 197 Wall Street, 732-222-9255

West Orange: Cycle Experts, 649 Eagle Rock Avenue, 973-731-9000

Westwood: Albert's, 182 Third Avenue, 201-664-1688

Westfield: Jay's Cycle Center, 227 North Avenue, 908-232-3250; Pro Tour Cycles, 405 South Avenue, 908-232-0430

Whippany: Whippany Cycle Shop Co., Inc., 971 State Route 10, 973-887-8150

Whitehouse Station: Garden State Bicycle, 470 US Highway 22, 908-534-1088

Williamstown: Bicycle Pro Shop, 604 Black Horse Pike, 856-875-8809

Willingboro: Burlington County Bicycle Center, 43 Charleston Road, 609-877-8016

Woodbridge: Bernie's Bicycle Store, 80 Main Street, 732-634-3938

Wyckoff: Bergen County Cyclery, 231 Everett Avenue, 201-891-3223

National Organizations

Adventure Cycling Association, 150 East Pine Street, Missoula, MT 59802; 406-721-1776. A national, nonprofit recreational bicycling organization providing access to more than 20,000 miles of bicycle route maps listing campgrounds, hostels, bike shops, restaurants, and other services a cyclist needs, in addition to a recreational cycling magazine, *The Cyclists' Yellow Pages,* and a variety of on- and off-road bicycle tours; annual membership fee.

Bicycle Coalition of New Jersey Cyclists, 7584 Remington Avenue, Pensauken, NJ 08110; 856-488-5843. A statewide bicycle advocacy organization.

Biking Is Kind to the Environment (B.I.K.E.), Box 667, Chatham, NJ 07928; 973-635-2211. A statewide bicycle advocacy group.

Hosteling International–American Youth Hostels, 891 Amsterdam Avenue, New York, NY 10025; 212-932-2300. A national organization that maintains a network of hostels and organizes bicycle trips. Annual membership fee, adults, youth, and senior citizens.

League of American Bicyclists, 190 West Ostend Street, Suite 120, Baltimore, MD 21230-3755; 410-539-3399. A nationwide organization of bicyclists that promotes bicycling by sponsoring annual races and maintaining a directory of bicycle route maps. Annual membership fee; includes monthly publication, *Bicycle USA.*

Lightwheels, 49 East Houston Street, New York, NY 10012; 212-431-0600. Promotes non–fossil fuel vehicles.

New Jersey Bicycling Association, c/o Cindy Donnelly, 416 Catherine Street, Somerville, NJ 08876; 908-725-8250. Association of New Jersey bicycle racing clubs.

New Jersey Conservation Club, c/o Wally Tunison, The Bicycle Hub, 455 Route 520, Marlboro, NJ 07748; 732-972-8822. An IMBA-affiliated New Jersey land access organization.

New Jersey Rails and Trails, PO Box 23, Pluckermin, NJ 07978; 732-249-3669. A nonprofit group dedicated to preserving abandoned rail corridors and converting them to trails.

Pedals for Progress, 86 East Main Street, High Bridge, NJ 08829; 908-638-4811. An organization that reconditions bikes to send to South America.

Transportation Alternatives, 92 St. Marks Place, New York, NY 10009; 212-475-4600. A nonprofit advocacy organization working for bicyclists' rights and reduced auto use.

US Bicycling Hall of Fame, 166 West Main Street, Somerville, NJ 08876; 908-722-3620. An organization dedicated to the establishment of a permanent institution devoted to the past, present, and future of bicycling in America.

Women's Cycling Network, PO Box 302, Coraopolis, PA 15108. A national clearinghouse for women cyclists. Membership organization offers seminars, workshops, rides, and a quarterly newsletter.

New Jersey Bicycling Clubs

Appalachian Mountain Club Bicycle Committee, c/o Michael Antanis, 150 Piersall Avenue, Jersey City 07305

Atlantic Bicycle Club, c/o Tom's Atlantic Cyclery, PO Box 330, Allenwood 08720; 732-291-2664

Bergen County Bike Club, c/o Al Calero, PO Box 471, Hillsdale 07642; 201-825-1524

Bicycle Touring Club of North Jersey, c/o Bette Bigonzi, PO Box 839, Mahwah 07430; 973-284-0404

Central Jersey Bicycle Club, c/o Howie Glick, PO Box 2302, Edison 08818; 732-225-HUBS

Central Jersey Cycling Team, c/o Mike Rosenhaus, PO Box 185, Neshanic Station 08853; 908-369-4522

Century Road Club of America, c/o Kopps Bicycle Shop, Princeton 08542; 609-924-1052

Chain Gang, c/o Kim Hess, PO Box 5118, Phillipsburg 18865; 610-837-4884

East Coast Bicycle Club of Ocean County, c/o Rich Baumann, PO Box 260, Bayville 08721; 732-269-9702

Family Cycling, c/o Barbara and Mel Kornbluh, RR 8, PO Box 319E, Grwynewood Drive, Bridgeton 08302; 609-451-6127

Fort Dix Bicycle Club, c/o Edie Fennimore, ATZD-GAC-CR, Bldg. 5201, Fort Dix 08864; 609-562-6667

G.S. Park Ridge Cyclesport, 1 Hawthorne Avenue, Park Ridge 07656; 201-391-5269

Hamilton Velo Club, PO Box H, Trenton 08691; 609-587-1320

Jaeger Wheelmen Club, c/o William Power, 35 Sunset Avenue, West Trenton 08628; 609-882-7956

Jersey Rock'n Road, PO Box 1027, Vernon 07462; 973-764-8079

Jersey Shore Touring Society, PO Box 8581, Red Bank 07701; 732-747-8206

Jersey Velo Sport, 231 Tall Pines Drive West, Sewell 08080; 856-468-7270

Millburn Chatham Wheelmen, c/o Pat Driscoll, 20 Main Street, Millburn 07041; 973-376-0001

Morris Area Freewheelers, c/o Jack Kelly, 31 Elizabeth Lane, Budd Lake 07828; 973-691-9275

Morris Velo Sports Club, c/o Chris Frost, 5 Rose Lane, Summit 07901; 908-522-1165

North Jersey Bicycle Club, c/o Mike Fraysee, PO Box 329, Glen Spey, NY 12737; 914-856-3335

Outbike of NJ Alternative Biking Club for Lesbian/Gay Cyclists, c/o Don Logan, 215 Clinton Place, Hackensack 07601; 201-488-6295

Outdoor Club of South Jersey Inc., c/o Donald Villanova, 583 Ridgewood Terrace, Mt. Laurel 08054; 856-235-2457

Park Avenue Cyclists, PO Box 49, Scotch Plains 07076; 908-889-8531

Pioneer Cycling Team, 810 River Road, Chatham 07928; 973-701-0180

PMK Cycling, Inc., c/o Ribin Snyder Bauer, 44 Broadway, Freehold 07728; 732-431-2832

Princeton Freewheelers, c/o Ed Post, 30 Wolfpack Road, Mercerville 07619; 609-890-8259

Pursuit Cycle Club, 95 Cornell Drive, Vorhees 08043; 609-768-0767

Ramapo Valley Cycling Club, PO Box 240, Oakland 07436; 973-831-6199

Ridgewood Cycle Club, Inc., 35 North Broad Street, Ridgewood 07450; 201-444-2553

Ride Rider Velo, 107 South Maple Avenue, Basking Ridge 07920; 908-630-0110

Sandy Hookers Triathlon Club, c/o Doug Rice, PO Box 186, Red Bank 07701; 732-842-4317

Shore Cycle Club, c/o Janet Reinhard, PO Box 492, Northfield 08225; 609-965-4823

Somerset Wheelmen, c/o Don Post, 106 Flanders Avenue, Somerville 08876; 908-281-0356

South Jersey Wheelmen, PO Box 2705, Vineland 08360; 609-863-6693

South Mountain Cycle Club, 119 South Orange Avenue, South Orange 07079; 973-763-0277

Spoke-N-Wheel, 564-A Union Avenue, Bridgewater 08807; 732-271-2555

Summit Cycling Club, c/o Bob Huber, 20 Whitby Road, Cherry Hill 08003; 856-424-1137

Team Reaction, c/o Steve Scheider, 2607 Route 31, North Clinton 08809; 908-638-4488

The Hub Club, c/o The Bicycle Hub, 455 Route 520, Marlboro 07746; 732-972-8822

The Hudson Cycling Club, 2468 Lemoine Avenue, Fort Lee 07024; 201-944-8787

Western Jersey Wheelmen, 41 Philhower Road, Lebanon 08833, 908-832-7361

Wheelmen, c/o Tom W. Green, 394 Griscom Drive, Salem 08079, 609-935-2491

Books

Bicycling Books

Cuthbertson, Tom. *The Bike Bag Book.* Berkeley, CA: Ten Speed Press, 1986. An amazingly tiny-sized book loaded with clear repair directions if you get stuck on the road.

Cuthbertson, Tom and Rick Morall. *Anybody's Bike Book.* Berkeley, CA: Ten Speed Press, 1990. An easy-to-read bicycle repair manual covering maintenance you can easily do by yourself.

Ferguson, Gary. *Freewheeling: Bicycling the Open Road.* Seattle: The Mountaineers, 1984. Well-presented facts on choosing a bicycle, caring for it, food for the road, camping, and more.

Marino, John. *John Marino's Bicycling Book.* New York: Houghton Mifflin, 1981. A basic guide to bicycling and physical fitness.

Sloan, Eugene. *All-Terrain Bicycles.* New York: Fireside Press, Simon & Schuster, 1991. Advice on choosing and using mountain bikes, including repair and riding techniques.

Sloan, Eugene. *The All New Complete Book of Bicycling.* New York: Simon & Schuster, 1985. Everything you want to know about choosing, using, and maintaining a bicycle.

van der Plas, Rob. *The Bicycle Touring Manual.* Mill Valley, CA: Bicycle Books, 1990. Good information on touring, with chapters on all the basics, from selecting a bike and other equipment to maintaining your gear on the road.

Weaver, Susan. *A Woman's Guide to Cycling.* Berkeley, CA: Ten Speed Press, 1990. The emphasis is on fitness and enjoyment, especially for the woman cyclist.

Nature Books

Brockman, Christan. *Trees of North America*. New York: Golden Press, 1968. An illustrated guide with complete details, making tree identification a joy.

Durrell, Gerald. *A Practical Guide for the Amateur Naturalist*. New York: Knopf, 1982. This beautifully written reference book will answer any questions you have about the birds, bees, flora, and fauna.

Mace, Alice. *The Birds Around Us*. San Francisco: Ortho Books, 1986. An enjoyable, informative, full-color guide to attracting, observing, identifying, and photographing birds.

Martin, Laura. *Wildflower Folklore*. Old Saybrook, CT: Globe Pequot Press, 1984. Information on 105 wildflowers: how each was named, medicinal value, culinary uses, myths, legends, and stories.

Peterson, Roger Tory. *A Field Guide to the Birds*. Boston: Houghton Mifflin, 1980. For cyclists who want to identify the chirping overhead.

Peterson, Roger Tory. *A Field Guide to Wildflowers of Northeastern North America*. Boston: Houghton Mifflin, 1975. During spring, this book will be extremely helpful in identifying the bright carpet of wildflowers along your route.

Petrides, George. *A Field Guide to Trees and Shrubs*. Boston: Houghton Mifflin, 1973. Worth buying if you want to identify trees en route.

Pough, Frederick. *Rocks and Minerals* (Peterson Field Guides). Boston: Houghton Mifflin, 1996. Enhance your bicycle trip by learning to identify the rocks and minerals along the way.

Robbins, Chandler. *Birds of North America*. New York: Golden Press, 1983. Learn to identify the birds you encounter on these tours.

Roberts, David. *Geology, Eastern North America* (Peterson Field Guides). New York: Houghton Mifflin, 1996. Learn to identify rocks, land formations, and more with this excellent, detailed guide.

Watts, Mary and Tom Watts. *Winter Tree Finder*. Berkeley, CA: Nature Study Guide, 1970. A handy pocket-sized manual for identifying deciduous trees in winter.

Waxman, Nahum (ed.). *Complete Field Guide to North American Wildlife,* eastern edition. New York: Harper & Row, 1981. A complete reference book with excellent illustrations.

Information on New Jersey

Cunningham, John. *This Is New Jersey.* New Brunswick, NJ: Rutgers University Press, 1996. All about the state's history, towns, historic sites, and counties.

Kulik, Stephen, et al. *Audubon Society Field Guide to the Natural Places of the Mid-Atlantic States* (Inland). New York: Random House, 1984. Maps, tours, and descriptions of places of interest to the nature lover.

McMahon, William. *South Jersey Towns.* New Brunswick, NJ: Rutgers University Press, 1973. Delightful anecdotes about the people and places in southern New Jersey.

McPhee, John. *The Pine Barrens.* New York: Ballantine Books, 1978. A sentimental look at New Jersey's most mysterious region.

Menzies, Elizabeth. *Millstone Valley.* New Brunswick, NJ: Rutgers University Press, 1969. The history of the Millstone Valley in text and photographs.

Menzies, Elizabeth. *Passage Between Rivers.* New Brunswick, NJ: Rutgers University Press, 1976. Captioned photographs detailing the history of the Delaware and Raritan Canal.

New Jersey Bicycling Information (c/o Bicycle Advocate, NJ Department of Transportation, 1035 Parkway Avenue, Trenton, NJ 08625; 609-530-4578). Information on bicycle clubs in New Jersey, addresses of county offices for maps, touring tips, and access restrictions.

Pierce, Arthur. *Iron in the Pines.* New Brunswick, NJ: Rutgers University Press, 1957. The history of iron manufacturing in the heart of southern New Jersey.

Schwartz, Helen. *The New Jersey House.* New Brunswick, NJ: Rutgers University Press, 1983. Photographs and details of the architecturally interesting houses found in the state.

Zatz, Arline. *Best Hikes with Children in New Jersey.* Seattle: The Mountaineers, 1993. Describes in detail 75 easy to difficult hikes throughout the state, ranging from 1 to 8 miles. Driving directions, historical descriptions, plus flora and fauna, what to take, and more.

Zatz, Arline. *New Jersey's Special Places.* Woodstock, VT: The Countryman Press, 1998. Fifty-two outings to New Jersey's most fascinating natural and historical attractions.

Maps

State road maps are available at state tourist centers and from the New Jersey Department of Commerce and Economic Development, Division of Travel and Tourism, CN 826, Trenton, NJ 08625. For additional tourist information, call 1-800-JERSEY-7. More detailed maps of each county are available free, or for a nominal fee, by calling the county offices listed below:

Atlantic: 609-645-7700

Bergen: 201-646-2900

Burlington: 609-265-5067

Camden: 856-783-0043

Cape May: 609-465-7111

Cumberland: 609-453-2192

Essex: 973-226-8500

Gloucester: 856-853-3271

Hudson: 201-795-6060

Hunterdon: 732-788-1227

Mercer: 732-989-6600

Middlesex: 732-745-3285

Monmouth: 732-431-7460

Morris: 973-326-7600

Ocean: 973-929-2130

Passaic: 973-881-4456

Salem: 856-769-1044

Somerset: 973-231-7024

Sussex: 973-579-0430

Union: 908-527-4744

Warren: 908-475-5361

Let Backcountry Guides Take You There

Our experienced backcountry authors will lead you to the finest trails, parks, and back roads in the following areas:

50 Hikes Series
50 Hikes in the Adirondacks
50 Hikes in Connecticut
50 Hikes in the Maine Mountains
50 Hikes in Coastal and Southern Maine
50 Hikes in Massachusetts
50 Hikes in Maryland
50 Hikes in Michigan
50 Hikes in the White Mountains
50 More Hikes in New Hampshire
50 Hikes in New Jersey
50 Hikes in Central New York
50 Hikes in Western New York
50 Hikes in the Mountains of North Carolina
50 Hikes in Ohio
50 Hikes in Eastern Pennsylvania
50 Hikes in Central Pennsylvania
50 Hikes in Western Pennsylvania
50 Hikes in the Tennessee Mountains
50 Hikes in Vermont
50 Hikes in Northern Virginia

Walks and Rambles Series
Walks and Rambles on Cape Cod and the Islands
Walks and Rambles on the Delmarva Peninsula
Walks and Rambles in the Western Hudson Valley
Walks and Rambles on Long Island
Walks and Rambles in Ohio's Western Reserve
Walks and Rambles in Rhode Island
Walks and Rambles in and around St. Louis

25 Bicycle Tours Series
25 Bicycle Tours in the Adirondacks
25 Bicycle Tours on Delmarva
25 Bicycle Tours in Savannah and the Carolina Low Country
25 Bicycle Tours in Maine
25 Bicycle Tours in Maryland
25 Bicycle Tours in the Twin Cities and Southeastern Minnesota
30 Bicycle Tours in the Finger Lakes Region
25 Bicycle Tours in the Hudson Valley
25 Bicycle Tours in Maryland
25 Bicycle Tours in Ohio's Western Reserve
25 Bicycle Tours in the Texas Hill Country and West Texas
25 Bicycle Tours in Vermont
25 Bicycle Tours in and around Washington, D.C.
30 Bicycle Tours in Wisconsin
25 Mountain Bike Tours in the Adirondacks
25 Mountain Bike Tours in the Hudson Valley
25 Mountain Bike Tours in Massachusetts
25 Mountain Bike Tours in New Jersey
Backroad Bicycling in Connecticut
Backroad Bicycling on Cape Cod, Martha's Vineyard, and Nantucket
Backroad Bicycling in Eastern Pennsylvania
The Mountain Biker's Guide to Ski Resorts

Bicycling America's National Parks Series
Bicycling America's National Parks: Arizona & New Mexico
Bicycling America's National Parks: California
Bicycling America's National Parks: Oregon & Washington
Bicycling America's National Parks: Utah & Colorado

We offer many more books on hiking, fly-fishing, travel, nature, and other subjects. Our books are available at bookstores and outdoor stores everywhere. For more information or a free catalog, please call 1-800-245-4151 or write to us at The Countryman Press, P.O. Box 748, Woodstock, Vermont 05091. You can find us on the Internet at www.countrymanpress.com.